PLAY and LEARN

Spanish

Second Edition

Ana Lomba *and* Marcela Summerville

Illustrations by Pedro Pérez del Solar and Corne Cartoons/Enroc Illustrators

McGraw Hill

New York   Chicago   San Francisco   Lisbon   London   Madrid   Mexico City
Milan   New Delhi   San Juan   Seoul   Singapore   Sydney   Toronto

ISBN   978-0-07-175928-1 (book and CD set)
MHID   0-07-175928-X (book and CD set)

ISBN   978-0-07-175926-7 (book for set)
MHID   0-07-175926-3 (book for set)

e-ISBN   978-0-07-178170-1
e-MHID   0-07-178170-6

Library of Congress Control Number   2011929606

Interior artwork copyright © by Pedro Pérez del Solar and Corne Cartoons/Enroc Illustrators
Interior design by Think Design Group LLC

McGraw-Hill books are available at special quantity discounts to use as premiums and sales promotions or for use in corporate training programs. To contact a representative, please e-mail us at bulksales@mcgraw-hill.com.

This book is printed on acid-free paper.

Contents

Track Listing

    Acknowledgments **1**

1   Introduction **2**

¡Buenos días! *Good Morning!*

2   ¡A levantarse! *Time to Get Up!* **8**

3   ¡A desayunar! *Time for Breakfast!* **9**

4   Vocabulario **8–9**

Listo para el día *Ready for the Day*

5   ¡Qué guapo/a estás! *You Look So Handsome!* **10**

6   ¡A vestirse! *Time to Get Dressed!* **11**

7   Vocabulario **10–11**

¡Vamos afuera! *Let's Go Outside!*

8   ¡Hace frío! ¡Hace calor! *It's Cold! It's Hot!* **12**

9   El ratón y los zapatos *The Mouse and the Shoes* **13**

10   Vocabulario **12–13**

¡Vamos a cocinar! *Let's Cook!*

11   Vamos al supermercado *Let's Go to the Supermarket* **14**

12   Vamos a cocinar juntos *Let's Cook Together* **15**

13   Vocabulario **14–15**

Hora de almorzar *Lunchtime*

14   El almuerzo *Lunch* **16**

15   La sopa loca *Crazy Soup* **17**

16   Vocabulario **16–17**

Hora de cenar *Dinnertime*

17   ¡Revolución en la cocina! *Revolution in the Kitchen!* **18**

18   La cena *Dinner* **19**

19   Vocabulario **18–19**

Por la cocina *In the Kitchen*

20   El postre *Dessert* **20**

21   A limpiar la cocina *Let's Clean the Kitchen* **21**

22   Vocabulario **20–21**

¡A bañarse! *Bath Time!*

23   ¡Al agua pato! *Duck, to the Water!* **22**

24   Toalla, esponja y jabón *Towel, Sponge, and Soap* **23**

25   Vocabulario **22–23**

¡Buenas noches! *Good Night!*

26   Vamos a la cama *Let's Go to Bed* **24**

27   La luna *The Moon* **25**

28   Vocabulario **24–25**

¡A jugar! *Playtime!*

29   El escondite *Hide-and-Seek* **26**

30   Vamos a recoger *Let's Put It Away* **27**

31   Vocabulario **26–27**

¡Vamos a ser bomberos! *Let's Be Firemen!*

32   Jugando a los bomberos *Playing Firemen* **28**

33   El camión de bomberos *The Fire Truck* **29**

34   Vocabulario **28–29**

Vamos a imaginar *Let's Imagine*

35   Las princesas *Princesses* **30**

36   Los piratas *Pirates* **31**

37   Vocabulario **30–31**

En el coche *In the Car*

38   En el taller mecánico *At the Auto Mechanic* **32**

39   En la gasolinera *At the Gas Station* **33**

40   Vocabulario **32–33**

Haciendo deporte *Playing Sports*

41   Jugando al fútbol *Playing Soccer* **34**

42   A saltar la cuerda *Let's Jump Rope* **35**

43   Vocabulario **34–35**

Yendo a sitios *Going Places*

44   Voy en bicicleta *I am Going on My Bicycle* **36**

45   El semáforo *The Traffic Light* **37**

46   Vocabulario **36–37**

¡Vamos al parque! *Let's Go to the Park!*

47   En el parque *In the Park* **38**

48   En los columpios *On the Swings* **39**

49   Vocabulario **38–39**

¡Vamos a sitios divertidos!
Let's Go to Fun Places!

50 En el zoo   At the Zoo   **40**

51 En el parque de diversiones
At the Amusement Park   **41**

52 Vocabulario   **40–41**

¡Vamos de museos!   Let's Go to the Museum!

53 En el Museo de Ciencias Naturales
In the Museum of Natural Science   **42**

54 En el museo de arte   At the Art Museum   **43**

55 Vocabulario   **42–43**

Visitando a la familia   Visiting Family

56 A casa de los abuelos
Going to Grandma and Grandpa's   **44**

57 Mi familia   My Family   **45**

58 Vocabulario   **44–45**

Los animales   Animals

59 En la granja   At the Farm   **46**

60 Los animales juegan   The Animals Play   **47**

61 Vocabulario   **46–47**

No me siento bien   I Don't Feel Well

62 Al doctor   To the Doctor's   **48**

63 El resfrío   The Cold   **49**

64 Vocabulario   **48–49**

¡Feliz cumpleaños!   Happy Birthday!

65 La fiesta de cumpleaños   The Birthday Party   **50**

66 La tarta   The Cake   **51**

67 Vocabulario   **50–51**

¡Vamos a la playa!   Let's Go to the Beach!

68 En la playa   At the Beach   **52**

69 Castillos de arena   Sand Castles   **53**

70 Vocabulario   **52–53**

En la primavera   In the Spring

71 Los movimientos de la primavera
Spring's Movements   **54**

72 La lluvia   The Rain   **55**

73 Vocabulario   **54–55**

En el verano   In the Summer

74 A pescar   Let's Go Fishing   **56**

75 Por el río   By the River   **57**

76 Vocabulario   **56–57**

En el otoño   In the Fall

77 Los esqueletos   The Skeletons   **58**

78 Una bruja mala   A Bad Witch   **59**

79 Vocabulario   **58–59**

En el invierno   In the Winter

80 La tormenta de nieve   The Snowstorm   **60**

81 El muñeco de nieve   The Snowman   **61**

82 Vocabulario   **60–61**

Uso tecnología   I Use Technology

83 Vamos a poner fotos en Facebook
Let's Post Pictures on Facebook   **62**

84 Hablamos con los primos
We Talk with Our Cousins   **63**

85 Vocabulario   **62–63**

En la ciudad   In the City

86 Año Nuevo en el barrio chino
New Year's in Chinatown   **64**

87 Comiendo en la ciudad   Eating in the City   **65**

88 Vocabulario   **64–65**

En la escuela   At School

89 El primer día de escuela
The First Day of School   **66**

90 ¡Vamos a hacer matemáticas!
Let's Do Math!   **67**

91 Vocabulario   **66–67**

Quiero a mis mascotas   I Love My Pets

92 Quiero un gatito   I Want a Kitty   **68**

93 Mi perro va a la escuela canina
My Dog Goes to Dog School   **69**

94 Vocabulario   **68–69**

Nos vamos de viaje   We're Going on a Trip

95 En el aeropuerto   At the Airport   **70**

96 En el hotel   At the Hotel   **71**

97 Vocabulario   **70–71**

Juegos   Games

98 En mi casa   In My House   **72**

99 En la clase de la señorita Calamidad…
In Miss Calamity's Class . . .   **74**

Acknowledgments

We would like to express our heartfelt thanks and appreciation to the many friends and colleagues who have encouraged and supported us along the way.

A special thanks is due to the following people, who have facilitated book production and design:

- Pedro Pérez del Solar, illustrator, for his magical ability to bring our stories to life

- Corne Cartoons/Enroc Illustrators, for the wonderful new illustratons in this second edition

- Rob Zollman, musician, for the recordings of the first edition, and for all the fun we had making them!

- Bonnie Blader, Ana's dear friend and unofficial proofreader, for her golden touch with language, adding flair to the English translation

- Karen Young, our editor at McGraw-Hill, who guided us through the process of writing this book with keen insight and friendly advice

We would also like to thank all those people in our personal lives who have made this book possible:

- Joseph, Victoria, Ana, Tyler, and Marina, our children, who are our constant inspiration

- Ozzie and John, our husbands, for their eternal patience—we couldn't have done it without you!

- Our readers and students, for being our best fans

This book is dedicated to Ana's beloved daughter, Marina, a special-needs child who reminds us every day of the miracle of learning.

Introduction

Young children are to language what ducklings are to water. Let them jump in and play!

—Ana Lomba

Welcome to a new edition of *Play and Learn Spanish*! It is because of forward thinking and visionary parents, grandparents, and educators like you that tens of thousands of children are now using *Play and Learn* to learn Spanish in early childhood—*the prime time for language learning.* Bravo!

You sent us e-mails, posted comments on our blogs, talked to us via social media, and we listened! As you will soon discover, we have included many of your great suggestions in this book.

In this new edition you will be able to:

• Listen to the picture vocabulary words and strips on each page.

• Focus on a scene at a time (no need to listen to the entire theme anymore!).

• Enjoy listening to professional voice-over talents (Marcela and I did our best, but we are certainly not voice professionals!).

In addition, not only will you learn new vocabulary through five new themes, but you will also:

• Learn how to scaffold language by playing two board games in Spanish.

• Learn how to teach like a pro with the strategies included in this introduction.

Ana Lomba's Easy Immersion® Method

There is plenty of research today showing that early childhood is the prime time for learning languages. We also know that young children learn languages best in interactive exchanges with their parents or teachers.

Unfortunately, over the last few years there has been a spike of flashcard-based foreign language programs especially targeted to young children. While your child may learn a few words and phrases from these programs, this type of approach is quite detrimental in the long run, as precious time is wasted on activities that do not lead to authentic real-life proficiency. Your child will learn much more in the context of playing and speaking with you!

Ana's breakthrough method ("Ana Lomba's Easy Immersion®") is based on three principles:

- Young children learn a new language best when they use it in everyday situations.

- Young children learn a new language best when they use it to interact with their parents, teachers, and friends.

- Young children learn a new language best when there is a bridge between the home and the school.

A large majority of the adults teaching Spanish or other languages to young children are not native speakers and do not hold degrees in language education (much less in early language education). This, however, should not be seen as an impediment to teaching languages. Moreover, it should not be seen as an impediment to teaching in an immersive way.

The fact that you are not fluent in Spanish or that you are a total beginner in Spanish does not mean that you can only teach words to your kids. It just means that you will need more support in order to do that. This is where Ana's Easy Immersion comes to the rescue. Ana's materials provide content and how-to knowledge for non-native and native parents and teachers who want to teach languages in a way that targets real-life proficiency.

Play and Learn Spanish and Ana's other materials are designed to assist parents and teachers who:

- Are serious about learning Spanish with their children.

- Look forward to the challenge and the rewards of learning a new language.

- Believe that they can be the initial motor that sparks their children's world language education.

The word "Easy" before "Immersion" does not mean that learning Spanish will always be easy. Instead, it is used to make a distinction between your experience using Ana's method from that of landing in a foreign country not speaking a word of the language—that would certainly be hard! As you will discover with *Play and Learn Spanish*, you will immediately understand the content and be able to use it with your children.

One final thought on Ana's Easy Immersion: when you start using this book, you may think that the recorded speakers talk too fast. This is to be expected! You are immersing yourself in authentic speech, after all. Give it time for the language to sink in and become your own. This is no different from listening to a song for the first time and trying to remember all the lyrics. Each time you will understand more, and soon enough you will be able to use the new language even in spontaneous conversations.

How to Use This Book

Start with the activities most interesting to your child. This program isn't based on a linear progression. Begin with the activity you think your child will enjoy and proceed as you wish. Some situations are easier and others more complicated; thus the activities and conversations accommodate different ages and language levels.

Use the illustrations as a picture dictionary. Visual input will help strengthen understanding, accelerate oral fluency, and facilitate emerging literacy in the new language. Read the captions at the bottoms of the pages while pointing to the pictures and then ask your child simple questions like *¿Cuál es el tenedor?* (Which one is the fork?), *¿Dónde está el tren?* (Where is the train?), or *¿Qué es esto?* (What is this?). Key Spanish words and expressions (and their English counterparts) in the activities, games, and songs are boldfaced to facilitate learning and help build new vocabulary. Children's lines in

song lyrics and responses in activities appear in *italics*.

Take it easy. We recommend taking baby steps. Don't try to learn everything at once. Follow your own child's learning rhythm. Start with the expressions or vocabulary words that you think will be most appealing to your child and then build by using the expressions in other situations as well.

Use the new language frequently. Set your own goals and work at your own pace. Your child will benefit from as little as fifteen minutes of Spanish three to four times a week. Please try to make these moments feel as natural and playful as possible and always follow your child's lead.

Don't let pronunciation stop you. Traditional language learning programs put too much emphasis on pronunciation, which has proven counterproductive again and again. Your pronunciation will improve as you go. Our goal is to help you to communicate with all Spanish speakers, not to speak with a perfect Castilian or Argentinean accent. Your children will have an advantage over you in pronunciation, as their young minds will be able to register sounds to which you have become deaf.

Make it a game. Your attitude is important. Young children respond better to exciting and playful endeavors than to formal "sit-and-recite" learning. Make learning Spanish a game.

Don't hesitate to use the new language in front of Spanish speakers. Why are you learning Spanish if not to speak with native speakers? Chances are you and your child will make new friends and will enrich your knowledge of the new language and culture.

Expand the learning experience. Consider creating a language corner for your child. The corner can include books, postcards, posters, and other culture-oriented items. If you have friends traveling to another country, ask them to bring you postcards, subway maps, menus, and other small souvenirs. Encourage your child to "teach" Spanish to other family members. In this way you can build beyond the exercises in this book.

Focus on your interaction with your child. The best way to learn a language is through personal interaction. Tapes, videos, and other materials will help, but they will never be enough. That is why we encourage you to speak to your child in Spanish. Never assume your child will effectively learn by simply parroting a tape or video.

Use the language naturally. Avoid constant translation and unnecessary explanations. If you translate to children, they will not make the effort to learn the new language. Use translation only if you see your child becoming frustrated.

Encourage but don't force speaking. Most children immersed in a second language pass through an initial "silent" period. While called "silent," it is not necessarily so, as children may respond in their first language. This is fine. Children need time to figure out the links between the new words and concepts, to understand, as well as to register and practice new sounds.

Don't be overly concerned about language "confusion." Mixing words, accents, and even grammatical structures is normal among young bilinguals. Contrary to common belief, this is not necessarily a sign of language confusion or of speech or language delay. Unfortunately, this common misunderstanding about language learning is the cause of much unnecessary sacrifice and suffering for families who are advised to drop the second language. If you are concerned about your bilingual child's language development, seek the help of a therapist who specializes in bilingual issues and educate yourself on the topic as well.

About the Language Used in This Book

One-on-one relationships. Our program focuses on one-on-one interaction to simplify learning and better respond to parental needs. While you will not learn plural verb forms at this point, learning them will be much easier and less confusing in the future. These activities can easily be adapted to teach a larger group of children by simply using the plural forms of the verbs.

One-way exchanges. In most situations, the parent is the only speaker. This is because children need a lot of input before they are able to speak, just as happens when parents speak to their children in their first language. Children begin producing utterances when they feel ready after hearing modeled speech.

Dialects. Just as with English, Spanish usage changes from country to country and even within each country. We have made an effort to use more general language while maintaining the oral accents and some authentic expressions of our native countries, Spain and Argentina. These differences in pronunciation will give you a taste of the various Spanish dialects that exist.

Gender. In Spanish, all nouns are either masculine or feminine. Most nouns ending in "a" are feminine and most nouns ending in "o" are masculine, but not always. Because articles must agree in gender and number (i.e., singular or plural) with the noun they modify, it is a good idea to look at the article to determine if the noun is feminine or masculine. The masculine singular articles are "un" and "el" (*un niño* = a boy; *el niño* = the boy). The masculine plural articles are "unos" and "los" (*unos niños* = boys or some boys; *los niños* = the boys). The feminine singular articles are "una" and "la" (*una niña* = a girl; *la niña* = the girl). The feminine plural articles are "unas" and "las" (*unas niñas* = girls, or some girls; *las niñas* = the girls). Spanish articles are used more frequently and differently than English articles are. For example, Spanish usually uses definite articles when talking about body parts or getting dressed. In English, however, a possessive adjective is preferred: *Mueve **la** mano* = Move **your** hand; *Me pongo **el** pantalón* = I put on **my** pants.

Most Spanish adjectives and nouns change endings to "a" for feminine and "o" for masculine. We have indicated this with slashes in the text (*guapo/a* = handsome; *rojo/a* = red). If you don't see the slash, then the adjective or noun is used as is for both genders (*cariño* = honey; *verde* = green).

"Teach-Like-a-Pro" Strategies for Teachers

While this book was initially created for parents, many teachers are using it as well. We appreciate our colleagues' trust and support, and we offer these strategies as our way to say, "thank you"! We hope you find them helpful!

- **Work on a theme, not on isolated activities.** For example, you could create a unit based on the theme of "Winter and Health." Young children tend to get sick a few times during the winter season, and this is a great opportunity to talk about germs, going to the doctor, washing hands, and many other topics related to the winter and health. Select scenes from the book connected to the theme.

- **Extend the theme and integrate subjects.** If you talk about Day of the Dead for a week and the next week about polar bears, your students will have a very hard time learning Spanish. They may remember a word here and there, but that's all. Instead, extend the topic for a few weeks and integrate content from other area subjects. For example, in a "Winter and Health" unit, they could learn numbers to take their friends' temperature (math and science), draw a snowman (art), and learn the names and functions for some parts of the body (science).

- **Work on all four language skills but focus on speaking.** Integrating listening, speaking, reading, and writing from the very beginning is the magic key to take you further sooner. For very young children, "reading" may mean that *you* read a story to them or that they pretend to read a book that they have memorized in Spanish. Writing may mean practicing small motor skills and scribbling. Older students could listen to the situations in this book (without reading) and try to figure out what is happening. Note, however, that nothing will motivate your students more than being able to speak, so make a point of practicing speaking every day. At the beginning, you could just ask them to repeat after you. To encourage independent speaking, ask frequent questions, especially of the "w" and "h" type (when, why, where, who, which, and how). Do all of this in Spanish, of course!

- **Establish a school-home connection.** Recommend resources such as *Play and Learn Spanish* and Ana's other materials to your students' families and encourage them to learn Spanish with their children. *No other formula is more powerful in early language education than the collaboration between teachers and parents.* That is why Ana's materials have been designed for use in school and at home.

We love hearing from families and teachers. If you are using *Play and Learn Spanish* let us know how you do!

¡A levantarse!

Time to Get Up!

¡Buenos días! ¡Es hora de levantarse!
Despierta ya, cariño. Ha salido **el sol**.
¡Es hora de levantarse! ¡Buenos días!
¡Uy **qué sueño**!
Despierta, cariño.
Mira, es de día. Ha salido el sol.
Sol, solecito, caliéntame un poquito,
Hoy y mañana y toda la semana.
¡Arriba perezoso/a!
Dame la mano.
¡Uy qué sueño!
Venga, vamos.
Ten cuidado con **los escalones**.
Despacio, eso es.
Vamos a **la cocina**.
¿Qué quieres desayunar?

Good morning! It's time to get up!
Wake up, honey. The **sun** is out.
It's time to get up! Good morning!
Oh, **how sleepy**!
Wake up, honey.
Look, it's daytime. The sun is out.
Sun, little sun, warm me up,
Today and tomorrow and all week long.
Up, lazy one!
Give me your hand.
Oh, how sleepy!
Come on, let's go.
Be careful with the **steps**.
Slowly, that's it.
Let's go to the **kitchen**.
What would you like for breakfast?

Did You Know?

"Sol, solecito" *is a traditional Latin American song. The diminutive ending* ito/ita *would be translated as "little" in English (sol, solecito/sun, little sun). Other examples would be* árbol *(tree) and* arbolito *(little tree) and* silla *(chair) and* sillita *(little chair).* Ito/ita *can also be used with personal names to denote familiarity and love:* Ana/Anita *(Anna/little Anna);* Roberto/Robertito *(Robert/Bobby);* Juan/Juanito *(John/Johnny).*

El sol

¡Qué sueño!

Los escalones

La cocina

8

¡A desayunar!

Es hora de desayunar.
Ayúdame. Vamos a poner la mesa.
Aquí está **el cereal**. *¡Qué rico!*
Aquí está **la leche.**
¿Qué más falta?
*Falta **el jugo de naranja**.*
¿Quieres jugo de naranja?
Aquí están **los tazones para el cereal**.
¿Qué más falta?
*Faltan **las cucharas**.*
¿Qué más falta?
*Faltan **los vasos** para el jugo.*
Aquí están los vasos para el jugo.
¿Cuál quieres, el verde o
    el amarillo?
El verde.
Muy bien. Todo listo.
Siéntate a desayunar.
¡Oh, no! ¡Se te cayó el jugo!
Toma, límpiate.

Time for Breakfast!

It's time to have breakfast.
Help me. Let's set the table.
Here is the **cereal**. *Very yummy!*
Here is the **milk**.
What else do we need?
*We need **orange juice.***
Do you want orange juice?
Here are the **cereal bowls**.
What else do we need?
*We need **spoons**.*
What else do we need?
*We need **cups** for the juice.*
Here are cups for the juice.
Which one do you want, the green one or
    the yellow one?
The green one.
All right. Everything is ready.
Sit down to eat breakfast.
Oh, no! You spilled the juice!
Here, clean yourself.

La leche

El tazón

La cuchara

El vaso

Listo para el día
Ready for the Day

¡Qué guapo/a estás!

Con agua muy limpita,
mi **cara** lavaré.
Con pasta y con cepillo,
mis dientes limpiaré.
Pon **la pasta de dientes** en
    el cepillo de dientes.
Lávate los dientes.
Chachachachachacha.
Ahora con **el peine**,
mi **pelo** peinaré.
Me miro en **el espejo**.
¡Guau! ¡Qué guapo/a que estaré!
¡Guau!, ¡Qué guapo/a estás!

You Look So Handsome!

With very clean water,
my **face** I will wash.
With toothpaste and a toothbrush,
my teeth I will brush.
Put the **toothpaste** on
    the **toothbrush**.
Brush your teeth.
Chachachachachacha.
Now with the **comb**,
I will comb my **hair**.
I look at myself in the **mirror**.
Wow! I will look so handsome!
Wow! How handsome you look!

Did You Know?

Constant correcting not only does not help in the language learning process, it actually interferes with it. A better way to help is to model. For example, if your child says "**Estoy** frío," just smile and say, "Oh, ¿**tienes** frío? Yo también." (Your child used the verb estar when the expression requires tener—"Oh, are you cold? I am too.")

La pasta de dientes

El cepillo de dientes

El peine

El espejo

¡A vestirse!

¡Hay que vestirse!
Miremos en el armario.
Veamos—**pantalones, faldas,
camisas, camisetas…**
¿Qué quieres ponerte?
¿Quieres la falda roja?
¿Estos pantalones?
¿La camiseta verde
o la camisa amarilla?
La amarilla.
Muy bien. Mete **un brazo.**
Mete otro brazo.
Mete **la cabeza.** ¡Ya está!
¿Y qué más? ¿**Los pantalones cortos**?
Bien. Agárrate a mí.
Mete **una pierna.**
Mete la otra pierna.
¡Ya está!
¡Ala, qué guapo/a!

Time to Get Dressed!

Time to get dressed!
Let's look in the closet.
Let's see—**pants, skirts,
shirts, T-shirts . . .**
What do you want to put on?
Do you want the red skirt?
These pants?
The green T-shirt
or the yellow shirt?
The yellow one.
Very good. Put in your **arm.**
Put in your other arm.
Put in your **head**. All done!
And what else? The **shorts**?
Good. Hold on to me.
Put in your **leg.**
Put in your other leg.
All done!
Wow, how nice you look!

Los pantalones

La falda

La camiseta

Los pantalones cortos

¡Vamos afuera!
Let's Go Outside!

¡Hace frío!
¡Hace calor!

It's Cold! It's Hot!

A ver qué tiempo hace hoy.
¡Uy qué frío hace! ¡Qué frío!
¡Hace mucho frío! ¡Hace mucho frío!
Me pongo **el suéter** porque hace
　　mucho frío.
¡Hace mucho frío! ¡Hace mucho frío!
Me pongo **el gorro** porque hace
　　mucho frío.
¡Hace mucho frío! ¡Hace mucho frío!
Me pongo **la chaqueta**.
¡Hace mucho frío! ¡Hace mucho frío!
Me pongo **los guantes**.
¡Hace mucho frío! ¡Hace mucho frío!
Me pongo **la bufanda**.

Vamos dentro ya. ¡Uy qué calor hace!
　　¡Qué calor!
¡Hace calor! ¡Hace calor!
Me saco la chaqueta porque hace calor.
¡Hace calor! ¡Hace calor!
Me saco la bufanda porque hace calor.
¡Hace calor! ¡Hace calor!
Me saco los guantes.
¡Hace calor! ¡Hace calor!
Me saco el gorro.
¡Hace calor! ¡Hace calor!
Me saco el suéter.

Let's see what the weather is like today.
Aah, it's so cold! How cold it is!
It's very cold! It's very cold!
I put on my **sweater** because it's
　　very cold.
It's very cold! It's very cold!
I put on my **hat** because it's
　　very cold.
It's very cold! It's very cold!
I put on my **jacket**.
It's very cold! It's very cold!
I put on my **gloves**.
It's very cold! It's very cold!
I put on my **scarf**.

Let's go inside now. Aah, it is hot!
　　How hot it is!
It's hot! It's hot!
I take off my jacket because it's hot.
It's hot! It's hot!
I take off my scarf because it's hot.
It's hot! It's hot!
I take off my gloves.
It's hot! It's hot!
I take off my hat.
It's hot! It's hot!
I take off my sweater.

El gorro

La chaqueta

Los guantes

La bufanda

El ratón y los zapatos

The Mouse and the Shoes

¡Venga nos tenemos que ir!
¿Dónde están tus zapatos?
Zapatos, ¿dónde están?
Estarán con el ratón.

Un ratón, ton, ton,
a **un zapato marrón** subió.
El zapato hizo, ton, ton,
y el ratón rodó y rodó.

Un ratón, ton, ton,
a **un zapato azul** subió.
El zapato hizo, ton, ton,
y el ratón rodó y rodó.

A **un zapato negro**.
A **un zapato blanco**.
¡Venga, nos tenemos que ir!
Ponte los zapatos. Átate los cordones.

¡Oh, no! ¡Que viene el ratón!
¡Corre, corre! ¡Que viene el ratón!

Come on, we have to go!
Where are your shoes?
Shoes, where are you?
They must be with the mouse.

A mouse, mouse, mouse,
went up a **brown shoe**.
The shoe went tap, tap,
and the mouse rolled and rolled.

A mouse, mouse, mouse,
went up a **blue shoe**.
The shoe went tap, tap,
and the mouse rolled and rolled.

Went up a **black shoe**.
Went up a **white shoe**.
Come on, we have to go!
Put on your shoes. Tie your shoelaces.

Oh, no! Here comes the mouse!
Run, run! The mouse is coming!

Un zapato marrón

Un zapato azul

Un zapato negro

Un zapato blanco

13

¡Vamos a cocinar!

Vamos al supermercado

Let's Go to the Supermarket

Vamos al súper.
We're going to the supermarket.

¿Quieres ir en **el carrito**?
Would you like to go in the **cart**?

Aquí está la lista.
Here's the list.

Necesitamos dos **pimientos verdes**.
We need two **green peppers**.

Toma, uno y dos. *Dos pimientos verdes.*
Here, one and two. *Two green peppers.*

Ponlos en el carrito.
Put them in the cart.

¡Ya está!
It's already there!

Necesitamos tres **cebollas**.
We need three **onions**.

Toma, una, dos y tres. *Tres cebollas.*
Here, one, two, and three. *Three onions.*

Ponlas en el carrito.
Put them in the cart.

¡Ya está!
It's already there!

¿Qué más?
What else?

Necesitamos **un ajo**.
We need **garlic**.

Toma, un ajo.
Here, a head of garlic.

Ponlo en el carrito.
Put it in the cart.

¡Ya está!
It's already there!

Necesitamos **una barra de pan**.
We need a **loaf of bread**.

Toma, una barra de pan.
Here, a loaf of bread.

Ponla en el carrito.
Put it in the cart.

¡Ya está!
It's already there!

Mantequilla, yogures y **huevos**.
Butter, yogurt, and **eggs**.

Ponlos en el carrito.
Put them in the cart.

Ya está todo. Vamos a pagar.
That's all. Let's pay.

Un pimiento verde

Una cebolla

Un ajo

Unos huevos

Vamos a cocinar juntos

Let's Cook Together

¿Me ayudas a cocinar?

Vamos a hacer pisto. *¡Qué rico!*

Primero hay que lavar los pimientos.

Toma, lávalos tú.

Ahora hay que abrirlos.

Quítale **las pipas**. Bien.

Córtalos en trozos pequeños, así.

Ahora vamos a lavar **los tomates** y **los calabacines**.

Sécalos. Bien.

Corta los tomates con el cuchillo de plástico.

En cuadraditos, así.

Corta los calabacines en cuadraditos.

Y ahora, ¡a freír!

Echa **aceite** en **el sartén**.

Will you help me cook?

We are going to make pisto. *Yummy!*

First we need to wash the peppers.

Here, wash them.

Now we have to open them up.

Take out the **seeds**. Good.

Cut them in small pieces, like this.

Now let's wash the **tomatoes** and the **zucchini**.

Dry them. Good.

Cut the tomatoes with a plastic knife.

In little squares, like this.

Cut the zucchini into little squares.

And now, let's fry them!

Put **oil** in the **pan**.

Did You Know?

Pisto is a tasty vegetable dish from Spain. To make pisto, sauté chopped onions, zucchini, garlic, and green and red peppers in a saucepan with olive oil. Add diced tomatoes, salt, and pepper and cook until you get a thick stew. Serve it cold or hot, as a side dish, or as an entrée.

Un tomate

Un calabacín

Aceite

Un sartén

Hora de almorzar
Lunchtime

El almuerzo

Lunch

¡A comer!

¿Qué hay para comer?

Hay **sopa** y **pescado**.

No tengo hambre.

Pues tienes que comer un poquito.

No tengo hambre.

Toma, la sopa. Pruébala. Sólo un
    poquito.

¿Qué es esto naranja?

Son **zanahorias**.

No me gustan las zanahorias.

¿Y qué es esto verde?

Son **guisantes**.

¡No me gustan los guisantes!

¿Qué es esto marrón?

Es **carne**.

No tengo hambre.

También hay **helado**.

¡Quiero helado! ¡Eso sí me gusta!

¡Pensé que no tenías hambre!

Come un poco de sopa y pescado
y te doy helado.

Time to eat!

What's for lunch?

Soup and **fish**.

I'm not hungry.

But you have to eat a little.

I'm not hungry.

Here, the soup. Try it. Only a
    little bit.

What is this orange stuff?

They're **carrots**.

I don't like carrots.

And what is this green stuff?

They're **peas**.

I don't like peas!

What is this brown stuff?

It's **meat**.

I'm not hungry.

There's also **ice cream**.

I want ice cream! That I like!

I thought you weren't hungry!

Eat a little bit of soup and fish
and I'll give you ice cream.

Did You Know?

In the Hispanic culture, lunch (el almuerzo) *is the main meal of the day. In some
countries, it is normal for the family members to meet at home for about two hours
to be together for this meal.* El almuerzo *consists of salad, appetizer, or soup
followed by the main dish and dessert. Sometimes the meal may be followed by
the* sobremesa, *a time to linger and talk over coffee or perhaps a drink.*

Las zanahorias

Los guisantes

La carne

El helado

La sopa loca

Crazy Soup

El mantel, los platos hondos,
    los platos llanos, la sopa,
el cucharón—¡Ya está!
¡A comer!
En la casa de mi tío
comen sopa con **cuchillo**.
¿Qué haces?
¿Comes sopa con cuchillo?
¡Ay, ay! ¡Qué loco estás!
¡Ay, ay! ¡Qué barbaridad!
En la casa de Ramón
comen sopa con **tenedor**.
¿Qué haces?
¿Comes sopa con tenedor?
¡Ay, ay! ¡Qué loco estás!
¡Ay, ay! ¡Qué barbaridad!
En la casa de mi hermana
comen sopa con **cuchara**.
¡Menos mal! ¡Una cuchara!
¡Ay, ay! ¡Qué rica está!
¡Ay, ay! ¡Quiero un poco más!
¡Más sopa, por favor!

Tablecloth, bowls,
    plates, soup,
ladle—All set!
Time to eat!
In my uncle's house
they eat soup with a **knife**.
What are you doing?
Do you eat your soup with a knife?
Ay, ay! How crazy you are!
Ay, ay! What a foolish thing!
In Raymond's house
they eat soup with a **fork**.
What are you doing?
Do you eat your soup with a fork?
Ay, ay! How crazy you are!
Ay, ay! What a foolish thing!
In my sister's house
they eat soup with a **spoon**.
Good thing! A spoon!
Ay, ay! How tasty it is!
Ay, ay! I want a little bit more!
More soup, please!

El mantel

Un plato hondo

Un plato llano

El cucharón

Hora de cenar

Dinnertime

¡Revolución en la cocina!

¡Ay, qué pasa en la cocina
que hay tanta revolución!
La olla grita y grita
que la cena ya está lista,
y la mesa no está puesta.
El plato llegó rodando
para sentarse a la mesa
y tuvo una gran sorpresa
al ver que no había mantel.
Muy asustada **la copa** gritó:
¡Yo soy para agua y no para sopa!
El cucharón, muy orondo,
le dijo al plato hondo:
Ven que te sirvo la sopa,
que tú no eres copa.
Tomar sopa no es sencillo
si es con **tenedor** y **cuchillo**.
Toma sopa con **cuchara**,
así no te ensucias la cara.
La panera muy asustada gritó:
¡Me ensucié con **una galleta**!
¡Aquí estoy para ayudarte!
—le dijo **la servilleta**.
¡Silencio!—gritó **la sal**—
esta revolución debe terminar;
que ya es hora de cenar.

Revolution in the Kitchen!

Ay, what happens in the kitchen
that there is such a revolution!
The **pot** screams and screams
that dinner is ready,
and the table is not set.
The **dish** arrived rolling
to sit at the table
and it had a big surprise
to see that there was no tablecloth.
Very scared, the **cup** screamed:
I am for water, not for soup!
The **ladle**, very puffed out,
told the soup dish:
Come, I will serve you the soup,
since you are not a cup.
Eating soup is not simple
if it is with a **fork** and a **knife**.
Eat soup with a **spoon**,
that way you won't get your face dirty.
Very scared, the **breadbasket** screamed:
I got dirty with a **cracker**!
Here, I will help you!
—said the **napkin**.
Silence!—screamed the **salt**—
this revolution must come to an end;
it is dinnertime.

Una olla

Una copa

Una panera

Una galleta

La cena

Dinner

¡Es la hora de cenar!
¡La cena está lista! ¡Sentarse a **la mesa**!
Hay **carne asada**
con **puré de papas** y **ensalada**.
¿Tienes sed?
Toma, un vaso de **leche**.
Tómalo despacio.
¿Tienes hambre?
Toma, un poco de
    pan con mantequilla.
Dame tu plato, por favor.
Un trozo de carne, un poquito de puré
y un poco de ensalada.
¿Necesitas un cuchillo para cortar
    la carne?
Toma, pero ten cuidado, no te cortes.
Si terminas todo, pero todo,
te doy **fresas con crema**.

It is dinnertime!
Dinner is ready! Let's sit at the **table**!
There is **roasted meat**
with **mashed potatoes** and **salad**.
Are you thirsty?
Here's a glass of **milk**.
Drink it slowly.
Are you hungry?
Here is a little
    bread with butter.
Give me your plate, please.
A piece of meat, a little bit of mashed potatoes,
and a little salad.
Do you need a knife to cut
    the meat?
Here, but be careful, don't cut yourself.
If you finish it all, and I mean all,
I'll give you **strawberries with cream**.

Did You Know?

This song has the rhythm of a payada. *The Argentine* gaucho *liked to show his talent as a* payador. *Accompanied by a guitar he improvised poems* (payadas) *about any proposed subject. When two* payadores *met, they made duels of* payadas *in which one of them tried to defeat the other. Those duels were called* payadas de contrapunto *(singing matches).*

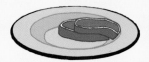

La carne asada

El puré de papas

La ensalada

Las fresas con crema

Por la cocina
In the Kitchen

El postre

¿Qué quieres de **postre**?

Hay **mandarinas, peras, uvas** y **plátanos**.

¿Quieres una mandarina?

Sí, una mandarina.

Vamos a pelarla.

Clávale la uña.

Así. Como yo.

Ahora, tira de **la piel** así.

Separa **los gajos**.

*Tiene **pipas**.*

Quítalas con la uña.

Está muy jugosa.

Toma, una servilleta.

Dessert

What do you want for **dessert**?

We have **tangerines, pears, grapes,** and **bananas**.

Would you like a tangerine?

Yes, a tangerine.

Let's peel it.

Stick your nail in.

Like this. Look how I do it.

Now, pull back the **skin** like this.

Separate the **slices**.

*It has **seeds**.*

Take them out with your nail.

It's so juicy.

Here's a napkin.

Did You Know?

Most people in Spain and Latin America eat fruit- or milk-based confections for dessert. The fruits offered change with the seasons. Adults may also have a cup of coffee or an herb infusion after dessert (never during the meal). The coffee is strong and served in small cups (like espresso). Water and wine are the main drinks served with lunch.

Una mandarina

Una pera

Unas uvas

Un plátano

A limpiar la cocina

Let's Clean the Kitchen

¡Qué sucia está la cocina! Vamos a
limpiarla.
Hay que poner los platos en
el lavaplatos.
Los platos van aquí abajo.
Los vasos van arriba.
Los cubiertos van en la cesta.
Hay que limpiar **la mesa**.
Toma, el trapo. Limpia la mesa.
¡Qué sucio está **el suelo**!
Vamos a limpiarlo.
Toma, **la escoba**.
Barre el suelo.
Toma, **el recogedor** para la basura.
Todavía está sucio.
Hay que fregar el suelo.
Toma, **la fregona**.
Friega el suelo.

The kitchen is so dirty! Let's
clean it up.
We need to put the plates in
the **dishwasher**.
The plates go down here.
The cups go up here.
Silverware goes in the basket.
We have to clean the **table**.
Here's the dishcloth. Clean the table.
The **floor** is so dirty!
Let's clean it.
Here's the **broom**.
Sweep the floor.
Here's the **dustpan** for the trash.
It's still dirty.
Now we have to mop the floor.
Here's the **mop**.
Mop the floor.

El lavaplatos

La escoba

El recogedor

La fregona

¡A bañarse!
Bath Time!

¡Al agua pato!

¡Es hora de bañarse!
La bañera está llena con agua tibia.
Déjame ayudarte a sacarte la ropa.
Uno, dos y tres. ¡Listo!
¡Al agua pato! Cua, cua, cua.
¡No me mojes!
Es hora de bañar a este **patito**.
Cierra **los ojos**, que te voy a tirar agua.
Un poco de **champú** para el pelo.
Rasco, rasco, rasco.
No abras los ojos todavía.
El pelo limpio.
¿Con qué lavo a este patito?
Aquí está **la esponja** y aquí está
      el jabón.
Te lavo **las manitas**.
Te lavo **la carita**.
Te lavo **la nariz**. ¡Ñam! ¡Me la comí!
¡Qué limpio está mi patito!
¿Con qué seco a mi patito?
Con esta **toalla** suavecita, suavecita.

Duck, to the Water!

It's bath time!
The **bathtub** is filled with warm water.
Let me help you take off your clothes.
One, two, and three. Ready!
Duck, to the water! Quack, quack, quack.
Don't get me wet!
It's time to bathe this **duckling**.
Close your **eyes**, I'm going to pour water on you.
A little bit of **shampoo** for your hair.
I scratch, scratch, scratch.
Don't open your eyes yet.
Clean hair.
With what do I wash my duckling?
Here is the **sponge** and here is
      the **soap**.
I wash your **hands**.
I wash your little **face**.
I wash your **nose**. Yum! I ate it!
How clean my duckling is!
What do I dry my duckling with?
With this soft, soft **towel**.

Did You Know?

¡Al agua pato (or patos)! is a common childhood bath-time expression in Spanish. Bath time is a great opportunity to teach your child the names of body parts. You may want to expand this activity by having your child bathe a doll. Model the behavior and encourage your child to take care of his or her "child" using Spanish words.

La bañera

El patito

El champú

La esponja

Toalla, esponja y jabón

Towel, Sponge, and Soap

Esta canción se canta con toalla,
    esponja y jabón.
Abrimos **la cortina**...
Abrimos **la canilla**...
¡Al agua cariño!
Así, así, así,
así me lavo el pelo.
Así, así, así,
ya me lo lavé.
Así, así, así,
así me lavo las manos.
Así, así, así,
ya me las lavé.
Así, así, así,
así me enjuago la cara.
Así, así, así,
ya me la enjuagué.
Así, así, así,
así salpico agua.
Así, así, así.
¡Uy! Un charquito formé.
Sal del agua, cariño.
Ven a secarte con esta **toalla**.

This song is sung with
    towel, sponge, and soap.
We open the **shower curtain** . . .
We turn on the **faucet** . . .
Into the water, honey!
Like this, like this, like this,
like this I wash my hair.
Like this, like this, like this,
I already washed it.
Like this, like this, like this,
like this I wash my hands.
Like this, like this, like this,
I already washed them.
Like this, like this, like this,
like this I rinse my face.
Like this, like this, like this,
I already rinsed it.
Like this, like this, like this,
like this I splash water.
Like this, like this, like this.
Oh! I made a little puddle.
Get out of the water, honey.
Come and dry yourself with this **towel**.

El jabón

La cortina de baño

La canilla

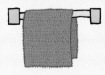

La toalla

¡Buenas noches!

Good Night!

Vamos a la cama

Let's Go to Bed

Vamos a tu **cuarto**.
Busquemos **un pijama** limpio.
Pero primero **un calzoncillo** limpio.
Toma, ponte este calzoncillo.
Primero un pie y luego el otro pie.
Toma, ponte este pijama.
Primero la cabeza, luego los brazos.
Ahora **los pantalones**.
Primero una pierna y luego la otra.
Ve al baño y cepíllate los dientes.
Cepíllalos bien, arriba y abajo.
¿Has hecho pipí? ¿No?
Haz pipí entonces.
Da los besitos de las buenas noches
y a **la cama**.
Toma tu **osito** y métete en la cama.
Ya te tapo.
Vamos a leer este **cuento**.
Había una vez una luna
que no quería dormir…

Let's go to your **bedroom**.
Let's find clean **pajamas**.
But first clean **underpants**.
Here, put on these underpants.
First one foot and then the other foot.
Here, put on these pajamas.
First your head, then your arms.
Now the **pants**.
First one leg and then the other.
Go to the bathroom and brush your teeth.
Brush them well, up and down.
Have you made pee pee? No?
Make pee pee then.
Give good-night kisses
and go to **bed**.
Take your **teddy bear** and get in bed.
Now I'll cover you.
We're going to read this **story**.
Once upon a time there was a moon
that didn't want to sleep . . .

Did You Know?

Reading foreign language books to your child three or more times a week is an excellent way to help him or her understand and develop new vocabulary. At first, choose picture books that use repetition, rhyme, and limited vocabulary. Then use the words and expressions learned in real-life conversation.

El cuarto

El pijama

El calzoncillo

La cama

La luna

La luna, la luna
salió de paseo,
en **una noche** clara
con su vestido nuevo.
Se miró en un charco.
Se vio muy hermosa.
Se pintó los labios
de color rosa.
Invitó a **una estrella**
a pasear esa noche,
pero la estrella le dijo:
Sólo si es en coche.
Invitó al sol,
pero **el sol** no quería,
porque sólo puede
salir durante el día.
La luna, la luna,
sola y aburrida,
se puso el pijama
y se quedó dormida.

The Moon

The **moon**, the moon
went out for a walk,
on a clear **night**
with her new dress on.
She looked at herself in a pond.
She saw she was beautiful.
She painted her lips
with the color pink.
She invited a **star**
to go out that night,
but the star told her:
Only if it is by car.
She invited the sun,
but the **sun** didn't want to,
because he could only
come out during the day.
The moon, the moon,
alone and bored,
put on her pajamas
and fell asleep.

La luna

La noche

La estrella

El sol

¡A jugar!
Playtime!

El escondite

Vamos a jugar al escondite.
Voy a esconder a tu perrito.
Tú cierra los ojos y cuenta.
Uno, dos, tres, cuatro, cinco, seis, siete,
   ocho, nueve y diez.
¡Abre los ojos!
Vamos a buscar al perrito.
¿Perrito, dónde estás?
¿Dónde estás, perrito?
"Guau, guau". ¡Lo oigo!
¿Estará detrás de **la cortina**?
No, no está aquí.
¿Estará debajo de **la mesa**?
No, no está aquí.
¿Estará detrás del **sofá**?
No, no está aquí.
Ya sé. ¿Estará dentro del **cajón**?
¡Sí, está aquí!
Ahora escóndete tú y yo cuento.

Hide-and-Seek

Let's play hide-and-seek.
I'm going to hide your doggy.
You close your eyes and count.
One, two, three, four, five, six, seven,
   eight, nine, and ten.
Open your eyes!
Let's look for the doggy.
Doggy, where are you?
Where are you, doggy?
"Bow wow, bow wow." I hear him!
Could he be behind the **curtain**?
No, he's not here.
Could he be under the **table**?
No, he's not here.
Maybe he's behind the **sofa**?
No, he's not here.
I know. Will he be inside the **drawer**?
Yes, he is here!
Now you hide and I will count.

Did You Know?

There are more bilingual than monolingual people in the world. A popular belief in monolingual countries is that the brain can only deal with one language, but research has shown that this is not the case. Quite the contrary, learning languages helps exercise the brain and build thinking and cultural flexibility. The quality of the education received is the key to success in any language.

La cortina

La mesa

El sofá

El cajón

Vamos a recoger

Let's Put It Away

Note: Repeat the *estribillo*/chorus after every other object that needs to be put away.

Estribillo:	Chorus:
Vamos a recoger.	We're going to put things away.
¡Qué lío!	What a mess!
A recoger tu cuarto ya.	We're going to clean your room now.
Vamos a recoger.	We're going to put things away.
¡Qué lío!	What a mess!
A recoger tu cuarto.	We're going to clean your bedroom.
¡Uy! ¡Qué lío!	Yikes! What a mess!
Vamos a recoger.	We are going to put things away.
¿Las muñecas dónde van?	*Where do the **dolls** go?*
Las muñecas en la cama.	The dolls go on the bed.
¿Los soldados?	*The **soldiers**?*
Los soldados en la caja. *(Estribillo)*	The soldiers in the box. *(Chorus)*
¿Los camiones?	*The **trucks**?*
Los camiones aparcados.	The trucks we have to park.
¿La comida?	*The **food**?*
La comida en la cocina. *(Estribillo)*	The food goes in the kitchen. *(Chorus)*
¿Los disfraces?	*The **costumes**?*
Los disfraces al armario.	The costumes in the closet.
¿El rastrillo?	*The **rake**?*
¿El rastrillo qué hace aquí?	What is the rake doing here?

Las muñecas

Los soldados

La comida

Los disfraces

¡Vamos a ser bomberos!
Let's Be Firemen!

Jugando a los bomberos

Playing Firemen

¡Suena la alarma! ¡Suena la alarma!	The alarm is ringing! The alarm is ringing!
¡Rápido! ¡Rápido!	Hurry! Hurry!
Vamos a bajar por **el tubo**.	Let's go down the **pole**.
Ponte **el traje**.	Put on your **suit**.
Ponte **las botas**.	Put on your **boots**.
Ponte **el casco**.	Put on your **helmet**.
Sube al camión. *¿Listo?*	Get in the truck. *Ready?*
¡Abran paso! *¡Abran paso!*	Clear the way! *Clear the way!*
Enciende **la sirena**.	Turn on the **siren**.
¡Vamos a apagar el fuego!	Let's put out the fire!
Toma **la manguera**.	Grab the **hose**.
Lanza **un chorro de agua**.	Blast a **stream of water**.
¡Arriba! Sube la escalera.	Up! Climb up the ladder.
¡Más agua! *¡Más agua!*	More water! *More water!*
¡Buen trabajo!	Great job!
El incendio se apagó.	The **fire** is out.

Did You Know?

You can make a fire truck with a large box. Use big paper plates for the wheels and small ones for the headlights and the siren. Make a hose with a vacuum-cleaner hose or a piece of water hose. Your child can wear a big bowl as a helmet, snow boots, and a big yellow or red shirt for the uniform.

El bombero

El casco de bombero

La manguera

Un chorro de agua

El camión de bomberos

The Fire Truck

¡Apúrate! *¡Apúrate!*
¡Vamos! ¡Vamos ya!
¡Vamos! ¡Vamos ya!
En **el camión de bomberos**.
En el camión de bomberos.
¡Apúrate! *¡Apúrate!*
Clang, clang, clang, clang.
Clang, clang, clang, clang.
¡Apúrate! *¡Apúrate!*
¡Sube **la escalera**!
¡Sube la escalera!
¡Apúrate! *¡Apúrate!*
¡Apaga **el fuego**!
¡Apaga el fuego!
Con mucha **agua**.
Con mucha agua.
¡Apúrate! *¡Apúrate!*

Hurry! *Hurry!*
Let's go! Let's go now!
Let's go! Let's go now!
In the **fire truck**.
In the fire truck.
Hurry! *Hurry!*
Ding, ding, ding, ding.
Ding, ding, ding, ding.
Hurry! *Hurry!*
Climb up the **ladder**!
Climb up the ladder!
Hurry! *Hurry!*
Put out the **fire**!
Put out the fire!
With a lot of **water**.
With a lot of water.
Hurry! *Hurry!*

El incendio

El camión de bomberos

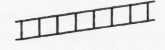

La escalera

El fuego

Vamos a imaginar

Las princesas

¿Quieres ser la princesa Blancanieves
o quieres ser Cenicienta?
Está bien. Ponte esta **corona**.
Ahora necesitamos **un caballero**.
Tú eres el caballero, ¿sí?
Usa la escoba como **caballo**.
Usa la regla como **espada**.
El sofá es **el castillo**.
Súbete al sofá.
¡Caballero, sálvanos!
¡Estamos atrapadas en **la torre**!
¡Mira, Cenicienta!
Allá, veo un caballero.
¡Gritemos!
¡Aquí, aquí caballero!
¡Nos ha visto! ¡Nos ha visto!
¡Mira! ¡Tiene una espada! Nos salvará.

Princesses

Would you like to be Snow White
or would you like to be Cinderella?
Okay. Put on this **crown**.
Now, we need a **knight**.
You are the knight, okay?
Use the broom as a **horse**.
Use the ruler as a **sword**.
The sofa is the **castle**.
Get on the sofa.
Knight, save us!
We are trapped in the **tower**!
Look, Cinderella!
There, I see a knight.
Let's scream!
Here, here knight!
He has seen us! He has seen us!
Look! He has a sword! He will save us.

Did You Know?

Once upon a time, Spain was a country of caballeros *(knights) and* castillos *(castles).*
The central part of Spain is called Castilla *(Castile), or "land of castles." The inhabitants*
of Castile are called castellanos *(Castilians), which is also the word for "lords of castles."*
The Spanish language (español) *is also called* castellano, *as the language of Castile.*
Today, Spanish is the language of twenty-two countries and their enchanting people.

Una princesa

Una corona

Un caballero

Una espada

Los piratas

Yo soy **el pirata** Barba Azul.
Aquí tengo **el mapa del tesoro**
   escondido.
El tesoro está en **una isla desierta**.
Mira el mapa.
Aquí esta **el barco**. ¡Todos a bordo!
¡A moverse! ¡Rápido!
Yo soy **el capitán**
porque tengo el sombrero más grande.
¡A moverse! ¡Vamos!
Comienza a remar,
   se viene **la tormenta**.
*Nos olvidamos de levantar **el ancla**.*
¡Qué viento! ¡A las velas!
La princesa Bella está llorando
porque tiene miedo.
Quiere un abrazo y un beso
pero los piratas no dan besos.
Muy bien, entonces ven a remar.
Vamos en dirección equivocada.
Vamos a dar la vuelta.
¡Tierra! ¡Tierra!
¡Veo la isla!

Pirates

I am the **pirate** Blue Beard.
Here I have the hidden
   treasure map.
The treasure is on a **desert island**.
Look at the map.
Here is the **ship**. All aboard!
Get moving! Quickly!
I am the **captain**
because I have the biggest hat.
Get moving! Let's go!
Start rowing,
   the **storm** is coming.
*We forgot to pull up the **anchor**.*
What a wind! To the sails!
Princess Belle is crying
because she's scared.
She wants a hug and a kiss
but pirates don't give kisses.
Okay, then come on and row.
We are going in the wrong direction.
Let's turn around.
Land! Land!
I see the island!

El mapa

El tesoro

Los remos

El ancla

En el coche
In the Car

En el taller mecánico

At the Auto Mechanic

El coche no funciona.	The **car** doesn't work.
¿Me ayudas?	Will you help me?
Vamos a arreglarlo.	*Let's fix it.*
Hace un ruido raro al arrancar.	It makes a funny noise when it starts.
Escucha: "¡Rrrrrr puf!"	Listen: "Rrrrr puff!"
¡Qué ruido más raro!	*What a strange noise!*
Vamos a mirar **el motor**.	Let's look at the **engine**.
Pásame **la llave inglesa**, por favor.	Pass me the **monkey wrench**, please.
Esto está bien.	This is fine.
Pásame **el martillo**.	Pass me the **hammer**.
Esto está bien.	This is fine.
Pásame **el destornillador**.	Pass me the **screwdriver**.
Esto no es tampoco.	This isn't it either.
Pásame **las tenazas**.	Pass me the **pliers**.
¡Anda! ¿Y esto qué es?	Oh, boy! And what is this?
Voy a tirar. Es un cable suelto.	*I'm going to pull. It's a loose cable.*
Vamos a hacer el plan dos.	Now for plan two.
Vamos a llamar a	Let's call
un mecánico de verdad.	a real mechanic.

Did You Know?

Living in another country is like driving a car for the first time. The language is the key to the car, but you also need to know what to do with it. If you don't, chances are you will be stuck in the driver's seat with no idea of what to do next. You'll experience culture shock. A good language program offers both language and culture.

La llave inglesa

El martillo

El destornillador

Las tenazas

En la gasolinera

Vamos a jugar a **la gasolinera**.
Ponte **la gorra**.
Lleno con súper, por favor.
*¿Con **tarjeta** o en **efectivo**?*
Con tarjeta. Toma.
*Abre **el depósito**, por favor.*
No llega **la manguera**.
Mueve el coche adelante.
Suficiente, gracias.
Ahora vamos a limpiar el coche.
Sube **las ventanillas**.
Yo traigo **el cubo** y **las esponjas**.
Frota bien **las ruedas**. Con más jabón.
Limpia **el polvo** de dentro.
Toma este **trapo**.
Frota bien **el volante**.
Ahora pasa **la aspiradora**
   por los asientos.
Vamos a enjuagar el coche.
Y ahora vamos a secarlo.

At the Gas Station

Let's play **gas station**.
Put on your **cap**.
Fill 'er up with super, please.
***Credit card** or **cash**?*
Credit card. Here.
*Open the **tank**, please.*
The **hose** doesn't reach.
Move the car up.
That's enough, thanks.
Now let's clean the car.
Roll up the **windows**.
I'll bring the **bucket** and the **sponges**.
Wipe the **wheels** well. With more soap.
Clean the **dust** inside.
Take this **cloth**.
Wipe the **steering wheel** well.
Now run the **vacuum cleaner**
   over the seats.
Let's rinse the car.
And now let's wipe it dry.

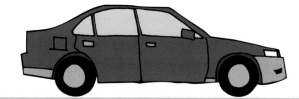

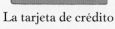

La tarjeta de crédito

Dinero en efectivo

La ventanilla

El volante

Haciendo deporte

Jugando al fútbol

¡Vamos a jugar al **fútbol** con
tus amigos David y Sonia!
Necesitamos **un balón** y **una portería**.
*David es **el portero**.*
*Vamos a meterle **un gol**.*
Venga, corre, pasa.
¡Gol! ¡Gooooool!
Ahora tú eres el portero.
Vete a la portería.
¡Venga, Sonia, pásame el balón!
¡Fuera de juego!
*Haz **un saque de esquina**.*
Dale con la cabeza.
Venga, corre, pasa.
¡Vamos a meter un gol otra vez!

Playing Soccer

Let's play **soccer** with
your friends David and Sonia!
We need a **ball** and a **net**.
*David is the **goalie**.*
*Let's score a **goal** on him.*
Come on, run, pass the ball.
Goal! Goooooooal!
Now you are the goalie.
Go to the net.
Come on, Sonia, pass the ball!
Out of bounds!
*Make a **corner kick**.*
Hit it with your head.
Come on, run, pass the ball.
Let's score another goal!

Did You Know?

Jump rope is still a very popular game among girls in Latin America and Spain.
You can play alone or in a group. It is best to start with the two rope turners moving
the rope from side to side while a third child jumps. This particular movement
is called saltar a la barca *(to jump the boat). The rope can also be moved in a*
whole circle.

El balón

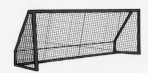

La portería

El portero

Fuera de juego.

A saltar la cuerda

Let's Jump Rope

Vamos a **saltar a la cuerda**.
Te toca dar. Una, dos y tres...
El nombre de María
que cinco letras tiene,
la M, la A, la R, la Í, la A:
Ma-rí-a.
Ahora el nombre de Begoña
que seis letras tiene,
la B, la E, la G, la O, la Ñ, la A:
Be-go-ña.
Ahora **el abecedario**.
A, B, C, D, E, F, G, H, I,
J, K, L, M, N, Ñ, O, P,
Q, R, S, T, U, V, W, X, Y, Z.
Ahora **las vocales**.
A, E, I, O, U
A...**amor**.
E...**eco**.
I...**indio**.
O...**oso**.
U...**uno**.

Let's **jump rope**.
It's your turn. One, two, and three . . .
María's name
has five letters,
M, A, R, Í, A:
Ma-rí-a.
Now, Begoña's name
has six letters,
B, E, G, O, Ñ, A:
Be-go-ña.
Now the **alphabet**.
A, B, C, D, E, F, G, H, I,
J, K, L, M, N, Ñ, O, P,
Q, R, S, T, U, V, W, X, Y, Z.
Now the **vowels**.
A, E, I, O, U
A . . . **love**.
E . . . **echo**.
I . . . **Indian**.
O . . .**bear**.
U . . . **one**.

La cuerda

Un indio

Un oso

Uno

Yendo a sitios
Going Places

Voy en bicicleta

I Am Going on My Bicycle

Vamos a montar en bici.
Ponte **el casco**—¡y nos vamos!
Vamos por **el parque**.
Hay mucha gente.
Vamos despacio.
Voy en bicicleta. Voy en bicicleta.
Voy en bicicleta por el parque.
Vamos por **carretera**.
Vamos rápido.
Voy en bicicleta. Voy en bicicleta.
Voy en bicicleta por la carretera.
Vamos por **el campo**.
¡Qué de baches!
Voy en bicicleta. Voy en bicicleta.
Voy en bicicleta por el campo.
Vamos por **el monte**.
Vamos para arriba.
Voy en bicicleta. Voy en bicicleta.
Voy en bicicleta cuesta arriba.
¡Y ahora para abajo!

We are going to ride our bikes.
Put on your **helmet**—and we go!
We are going through the **park**.
There are lots of people.
Let's go slowly.
I'm riding my bike. I'm riding my bike.
I'm riding my bike through the park.
We are going on the **road**.
Let's go quickly.
I'm riding my bike. I'm riding my bike.
I'm riding my bike on the road.
We are going through the **countryside**.
There are so many bumps!
I'm riding my bike. I'm riding my bike.
I'm riding my bike through the countryside.
We are going up the **mountain**.
Let's go uphill.
I'm riding my bike. I'm riding my bike.
I'm riding my bike uphill.
And now downhill!

Did You Know?

These are great games to play indoors. Sit on the floor and start "pedaling." Jump up and down when hitting a "bump," stick your tongue out and pretend to be out of breath when "going uphill," and scream when "going downhill." You can make a "traffic light" with cardboard and green, yellow, and red cellophane paper. Use a flashlight to simulate turning the lights on and off.

El casco

La carretera

El campo

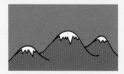

El monte

El semáforo

The Traffic Light

Súbete al **coche**.
Abróchate **el cinturón**—¡y nos vamos!
Mira **el semáforo**.
¡Luz verde! ¡Luz verde!
¿Qué hago?
Voy deprisa, deprisa, deprisa.
¡Pi, pi! ¡Mock, mock!
¡Luz amarilla! ¡Luz amarilla!
¿Qué hago?
Voy despacio, despacio, muy despacio.
¡Luz roja! ¡Luz roja!
¿Qué hago?
Me paro.

Get in the **car**.
Buckle your **belt**—and we go!
Look at the **traffic light**.
Green light! Green light!
What do I do?
I go fast, fast, fast.
Beep, beep! Honk, honk!
Yellow light! Yellow light!
What do I do?
I go slowly, slowly, very slowly.
Red light! Red light!
What do I do?
I stop.

El coche

Luz verde

Luz amarilla

Luz roja

¡Vamos al parque!

Let's Go to the Park!

En el parque

Hemos llegado al **parque**.
¿Quieres ir al **tobogán**?
Venga, sube.
Uno, dos, tres, cuatro, cinco, seis.
Muy bien, siéntate ahora.
Agárrate bien y ¡baja!
¿Quieres ir a **las barras**?
Venga, sube.
Uno, dos, tres, cuatro, cinco, seis.
¿Quieres ir a **la torre**?
Venga, sube.
Uno, dos, tres, cuatro, cinco, seis.

In the Park

We have arrived at the **park**.
Would you like to go on the **slide**?
Come on, go up.
One, two, three, four, five, six.
Very good, sit down now.
Hold on tight and go down!
Would you like to go to the **monkey bars**?
Come on, go up.
One, two, three, four, five, six.
Would you like to go to the **tower**?
Come on, go up.
One, two, three, four, five, six.

Did You Know?

La merienda *is a snack that many people in Spanish-speaking countries eat at around 5:00 P.M., after children come back from school. In Spain,* la merienda *consists normally of* bocadillos *(sandwiches made out of baguette bread) and milk chocolate for the kids and pastries and coffee or tea for the adults. Dinner in most countries is eaten at around 9:00 or 10:00 P.M., so an afternoon snack is always welcome.*

El parque

El tobogán

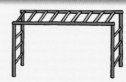

Las barras

La torre

En los columpios

On the Swings

Vamos a **los columpios**.	Let's go to the **swings**.
¿Te empujo?	Shall I push you?
¡Ahí vas!	There you go!
¡Más fuerte!	*Harder!*
¿Por qué no te das tú solo?	Why don't you push yourself?
A ver, levanta las piernas.	Let's see, pump your legs forward.
Ahora lleva las piernas detrás.	Now pump your legs back.
Así, delante, detrás.	Like that, forward, back.
Delante, detrás.	*Forward, back.*
¿Quieres parar?	Do you want to stop?
Vamos al **sube y baja**.	Let's go to the **seesaw**.
Está ocupado. Tenemos que esperar.	It's full. We'll have to wait.
¿Tienes hambre?	Are you hungry?
Te he traído	I brought you
un bocadillo de jamón serrano.	a **serrano ham sandwich**.

El columpio

El sube y baja

El bocadillo

El jamón

¡Vamos a sitios divertidos!
Let's Go to Fun Places!

En el zoo

Estamos en **el zoo**. Estamos en el zoo.
Veo los leones. Estamos en el zoo.
Los leones dicen, "Grrrr".
El león está durmiendo.
Allí está **la leona**.
El león tiene **melena** y la leona no.
Las jirafas están allí.
¡Qué **cuello** más largo tienen!
Las patas son muy largas también.
Los elefantes están allí.
¡Qué **orejas** más grandes tienen!
Mira como agarran los cacahuetes
    con **la trompa**.
Mira, los tigres.
¡Qué **bocas** más grandes tienen!
¡Mira, **los osos**!
Son muy grandes.
Mira, aquí están **las serpientes**.
Las serpientes dicen, "Ssss".
Son muy largas.

At the Zoo

We are in the **zoo**. We are in the zoo.
I see the lions. We are in the zoo.
The lions say, "Grrrrr."
The **lion** is sleeping.
The **lioness** is over there.
The lion has a **mane** and the lioness doesn't.
*The **giraffes** are over there.*
What long **necks** they have!
Their **legs** are very long, too.
*The **elephants** are over there.*
What big **ears** they have!
Look how they get the peanuts
    with their **trunk**.
*Look, the **tigers**.*
What large **mouths** they have!
Look, the **bears**!
They are very big.
Look, here are the **snakes**.
The snakes say, "Ssss."
They are very long.

Did You Know?

Spanish is the third most widely spoken language in the world after Mandarin Chinese and English. As with any major language, Spanish is used differently from country to country and even within each country. For example, the term Ferris wheel *is called* la noria *in Spain,* la rueda de la fortuna *in México and Chile,* la rueda moscovita *in Ecuador, and* la vuelta al mundo *in Argentina.*

El león y la leona

La jirafa

El elefante

El tigre

En el parque de diversiones

At the Amusement Park

Vamos a comprar **los tickets**.	Let's buy the **tickets**.
¿Dónde te quieres subir?	Which ride do you want to go on?
*En **la rueda**.*	*On the **Ferris wheel**.*
Vamos a sentarnos. Siéntate aquí.	Let's sit down. Sit here.
Dale el ticket a la señora.	Give the ticket to the lady.
¡Ala! ¡Qué alto!	*Wow! How high!*
¿Quieres ir al **carrusel**?	Would you like to go on the **merry-go-round**?
Te subo al **caballo**. ¡Arriba!	I'll get you up on the **horse**. Up!
Agárrate bien. Así.	Hold on tight. Like this.
Yo te sujeto, no te preocupes.	I will hold you, don't worry.
Dale el ticket al señor.	Give the ticket to the man.
¿Dónde quieres ir ahora?	Where would you like to go now?
*A **los coches de choque**.*	*To the **bumper cars**.*
Corre, vamos al coche rojo. Súbete.	Run, let's go to the red car. Get in.
Yo voy contigo, no te preocupes.	I'll go with you, don't worry.
Conduce tú.	You drive.
La montaña rusa.	*The **roller coaster**.*
¡Eso cuando seas mayor!	We'll do that when you are older!

La rueda

El carrusel

Los coches de choque

La montaña rusa

¡Vamos de museos!

Let's Go to the Museum!

En el Museo de Ciencias Naturales

In the Museum of Natural Science

Ven, creo que **los dinosaurios** están en esta sala.

*Es **un tiranosaurio**.*

¡Es gigante!

Los tiranosaurios se comían a otros dinosaurios.

Eran **carnívoros**.

Tenían **los dientes** muy afilados.

Mira, **una huella de un braquiosaurio**.

¡Es enorme!

Los braquiosaurios eran enormes, pero comían hojas de árboles.

Eran **herbívoros**.

Mira, **un estegosaurio**.

Los estegosaurios tenían cabezas muy pequeñas.

Come, I think the **dinosaurs** are in this room.

*It's a **tyrannosaurus**.*

It's huge!

Tyrannosauruses ate other dinosaurs.

They were **carnivores**.

They had very sharp **teeth**.

Look, a **brachiosaurus footprint**.

It's enormous!

Brachiosauruses were enormous, but they ate tree leaves.

They were **herbivores**.

Look, it's a **stegosaurus**.

Stegosauruses had small heads.

Did You Know?

Argentina is an important destination for paleontologists. The region of Patagonia is home to some of the oldest, biggest, and most unique dinosaurs in the world. About forty species of dinosaurs have been found in Argentina. This represents about 10 percent of all of the species found around the world. Among them are the Argentinosaurus, a plant eater that may be the largest dinosaur on earth, and the Gigantosaurus, the largest meat eater ever found.

Un tiranosaurio

Una huella

Un braquiosaurio

Un estegosaurio

Ponte la bata.

¿Qué vas a pintar?

Pon pintura en la paleta.

En el museo de arte

At the Art Museum

Vamos a ver la sala de Dalí.	Let's go to see Dali's hall.
Dalí era un artista español.	Dali was a Spanish artist.
*Mira este **cuadro**.*	*Look at this **painting**.*
Hay tres caras escondidas.	There are three hidden faces.
¿Las ves?	Can you see them?
Vete más lejos. ¿Ves las caras?	Go further. Do you see the faces?
Son un niño, un joven	They are a child, a young person,
y un anciano.	and an old person.
"Las tres edades".	**"The Three Ages."**
Ven por aquí.	Come this way.
Ésta es **una escultura** de	This is a **sculpture** by
Fernando Botero,	Fernando Botero,
un escultor y **pintor** colombiano.	a Colombian sculptor and **painter**.
Mira, tienen un taller de pintura.	Look, they have a painting workshop.
Coge **un pincel**.	Get a **brush**.
Ponte **la bata**. Espera, te ato.	Put on a **robe**. Wait, I'll tie you.
Ahora **las pinturas**.	Now the **paints**.
¿Cuáles quieres?	Which ones do you want?
¿Qué vas a pintar?	What are you going to paint?
Pon un poco de pintura en **la paleta**.	Put a little bit of paint on the **palette**.
Ahora toca la pintura con el pincel.	Now touch the paint with the brush.

Un cuadro

Una escultura

Un pincel

Una paleta

Visitando a la familia
Visiting Family

A casa de los abuelos

Vamos a casa de **los abuelos**.
Es **su aniversario**.
Vamos a comer
  panqueques de dulce de leche.
¡Qué ricos!
La tía Simona y **el tío** Antonio van a ir,
y también **la prima** Isabel, tu favorita.
Pero tienes que jugar también con
  el primo Juan.
¡Ya llegamos! Baja del coche.
Saluda a todos.
Dale un beso y un abrazo a la abuela.
¡Feliz aniversario!

Going to Grandma and Grandpa's

We are going to **grandma and grandpa's** house.
It's their **anniversary**.
We are going to eat
  sweet-milk **crepes**.
How delicious!
Aunt Simona and **Uncle** Antonio will be there,
and also your **cousin** Isabel, your favorite.
But you will have to play with
  your **cousin** Juan as well.
We arrived! Get out of the car.
Greet everybody.
Give your grandma a kiss and a hug.
Happy anniversary!

Did You Know?

Panqueques de dulce de leche *are among Argentines' favorite desserts. They are very easy to make. You can use any crepe recipe, but make sure the crepes are very thin. Spread the crepes with* dulce de leche *and roll them in a cylinder. Serve them warm. Dulce de leche *can be found in Latino stores and in many large supermarkets.*

Los abuelos

Los tíos

Los primos

Papá y Mamá

Mi familia

My Family

Yo tengo **una abuela**
que se llama Josefina,
que cuando **está contenta**,
se la pasa en la cocina.
Yo tengo **un abuelo**
que se llama Valentín,
que cuando **está enojado**,
se la pasa en el jardín.
Yo tengo **una tía**
que se llama Nicolasa,
que cuando **está cansada**,
se la pasa en la casa.
Yo tengo **un tío**
que se llama José,
que cuando **está triste**,
se la pasa en el café.
Yo tengo **una hermana**
que se llama Susana,
que cuando **está aburrida**,
se la pasa en la ventana.
¡Uy! Y también tengo
a mi **papá** y a mi **mamá**.

I have a **grandmother**
whose name is Josefina;
when she **is happy**,
she spends her time in the kitchen.
I have a **grandfather**
whose name is Valentín;
when he **is angry**,
he spends his time in the garden.
I have an **aunt**
whose name is Nicolasa;
when she **is tired**,
she spends her time in the house.
I have an **uncle**
whose name is José;
when he **is sad**,
he spends his time in the coffee shop.
I have a **sister**
whose name is Susana;
when she **is bored**,
she spends her time at the window.
Uh, oh! And I also have
my **father** and my **mother**.

Estoy contento/a.

Estoy cansado/a.

Estoy triste.

Estoy aburrido/a.

Los animales
Animals

En la granja

Ya hemos llegado a **la granja**.
Aquí están **las gallinas**.
Las gallinas dicen, "Co, co, co".
Aquí están **los pavos**.
Los pavos dicen, "Glo, glo, glo".
Mira, **el gallo** está arriba en el techo.
El gallo dice, "¡Kikirikí!"
¿Quieres echarle migas a **los pollitos**?
Los pollitos dicen, "Pío, pío, pío".
Vamos a ver **los caballos**.
El potro está con su mamá, **la yegua**.
El caballo es el papá.
¿Quieres ver **las vacas**?
El toro es el papá,
la vaca es la mamá
y **el ternero** es el bebé.
Mira, el ternerito está mamando.
Está bebiendo leche de su mamá.

At the Farm

We have arrived at the **farm**.
Here are the **hens**.
The hens say, "Cluck, cluck, cluck."
Here are the **turkeys**.
The turkeys say, "Gobble, gobble, gobble."
Look, the **rooster** is up on the roof.
The rooster says, "Cock-a-doodle-doo!"
Would you like to throw crumbs to the **chicks**?
The chicks say, "Peep, peep, peep."
Let's go to see the **horses**.
The **foal** is with his mom, the **mare**.
The **stallion** is the dad.
You want to see the **cows**?
The **bull** is the dad,
the **cow** is the mom,
and the **calf** is the baby.
Look, the little calf is nursing.
He's drinking milk from his mom.

Did You Know?

We inserted more animals and actions into this traditional song from Spain, "Los animales de la creación" ("The Animals of Creation"). This is a great song to play outdoors or indoors. Introduce the animals with illustrations or puppets and "dance" in a circle, imitating their movements.

Una granja

Una gallina

Un caballo

Una vaca

Los animales juegan

The Animals Play

Los pajaritos que van por el aire
vuelan, vuelan, vuelan, vuelan, vuelan.
Los pececitos que van por el agua
nadan, nadan, nadan, nadan, nadan.
Unos y otros bajo el sol,
unos y otros juegan como yo.
Los caballitos que van por el monte
corren, corren, corren, corren, corren.
Los conejitos que van por el campo
saltan, saltan, saltan, saltan, saltan.
Unos y otros bajo el sol,
unos y otros juegan como yo.
Las culebritas que van por el suelo
reptan, reptan, reptan, reptan, reptan.
Las ardillitas que van por el árbol
trepan, trepan, trepan, trepan, trepan.
Unos y otros bajo el sol,
unos y otros juegan como yo.

The **little birds** that go by air
fly, fly, fly, fly, fly.
The **little fish** that go by water
swim, swim, swim, swim, swim.
These and those under the sun,
these and those play like me.
The **little horses** that go by the mountain
run, run, run, run, run.
The **little rabbits** that go by the field
jump, jump, jump, jump, jump.
These and those under the sun,
these and those play like me.
The **little snakes** that go by the ground
slither, slither, slither, slither, slither.
The **little squirrels** that go by tree
climb, climb, climb, climb, climb.
These and those under the sun,
these and those play like me.

El pájaro

El pez

El conejo

La ardilla

No me siento bien
I Don't Feel Well

Al doctor

¡Ay! ¡Vaya **tos**!

Dime, ¿qué te duele?

¿Te duele **la garganta**?

Abre la boca grande, grande.

Di aaaaaaa bien fuerte.

¡Muy bien!

La garganta está inflamada.

¿Te duelen los oídos?

A ver este **oído**.

Este oído está bien. A ver éste.

¡Oh, oh! ¡Éste está infectado!

¡Qué de **mocos**!

Toma, **un pañuelo**.

Suénate **la nariz**.

¡Qué **resfrío** te pescaste!

Ponte **el termómetro**.

Tienes **fiebre**.

Toma **una cucharada** de este **jarabe**
dos veces al día.

Bebe mucho agua.

Vuelve en una semana.

¡Que te mejores!

To the Doctor's

Oh! What a **cough**!

Tell me, what hurts?

Does your **throat** hurt?

Open your mouth wide, wider.

Say ahhhhhh very loud.

Very good!

Your throat is inflamed.

Do your ears hurt?

Let me see this **ear**.

This ear is okay. Let's see this one.

Uh, oh! This one is infected!

What a **runny nose**!

Here, a **tissue**.

Blow your **nose**.

What a **cold** you have!

Put in the **thermometer**.

You have a **fever**.

Take a **tablespoon** of this **syrup**
two times a day.

Drink a lot of water.

Come back in a week.

Get well!

Did You Know?

Different languages reflect different cultures and different ways of understanding daily life. That is why literal translations can sometimes be linguistically correct but culturally inappropriate. For example, while most Spanish and Latin American parents would use the word mocos (mucus) *with their young children, English-speaking parents would say* runny nose. *The reverse may be true with other expressions.*

La garganta
inflamada

El oído

Los mocos

La nariz roja

El resfrío

Temprano esta mañana,
el niño se levantó,
con **dolor de garganta**
y con mucha tos.
Cof, cof, cof, cof.
¡Ay! ¡Pobre niñito!
¡Qué resfriado está!
Estornudó otra vez.
¡Achís, achís, achís!
Le lloran los ojos,
le pica la nariz.
La mamá le trae
un jarabe gris.
¡Achís, achís, achís!
¡Ay! ¡Pobre niñito!
¡Qué resfriado está!
Estornudó otra vez.
¡Achís, achís, achís!

The Cold

Early this morning,
the boy got up,
with a **sore throat**
and coughing a lot.
Cough, cough, cough, cough.
Ay! Poor little boy!
What a cold he has!
He sneezed again.
Achoo, achoo, achoo!
His eyes are watering,
his nose is itchy.
His mother brings him
a gray syrup.
Achoo, achoo, achoo!
Ay! Poor little boy!
What a cold he has!
He sneezed again.
Achoo, achoo, achoo!

El termómetro 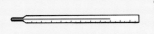 Una cucharada  El jarabe   Los ojos llorosos

¡Feliz cumpleaños!

Happy Birthday!

La fiesta de cumpleaños

¿Cuántos años cumples?

¿Seis? Eres un/a señor/a.

Dame tu oreja. Uno, dos, tres, cuatro,

cinco, seis y siete de propina.

¿Y tú cuántos años tienes?

¿Siete y medio?

¡Qué mayor eres!

Toma tus **regalos**. Ábrelos.

¡Venga, ábrelos!

*¡Es **un helicóptero**!*

¡Y esto también! Ábrelo.

A ver. ¿Qué es?

Un barco de piratas.

¡Niños, la tarta!

The Birthday Party

How old are you?

Six? You are a grown-up.

Give me your ear. One, two, three, four,

five, six, and seven is your tip.

And how old are you?

Seven-and-a-half?

You are so old!

Take your **gifts**. Open them.

Come on, open them!

*It's a **helicopter**!*

And this too! Open it.

Let's see. What is it?

*It's a **pirate boat**.*

Kids, the cake!

Did You Know?

In Spain and many Latin American countries it is customary to pull the birthday kid's ears. Traditions vary from country to country. In Mexico, for example, a party is not a party without a piñata. Many Latin American countries have big fifteenth birthday celebrations for girls.

Un regalo

Un helicóptero

Un barco

Un pirata

La tarta

The Cake

¡Ya viene **la tarta**! ¡La tarta!	The **cake** is coming! Cake!
¡Ya viene la tarta!	The cake is coming!
¡Vengan todos!	Everybody, come!
Siéntate aquí.	Sit here.
¡Las luces!	Lights!
¡Apaguen las luces, por favor!	Turn off the lights, please!
Vamos a cantar. Uno, dos y tres.	Let's sing. One, two, and three.
Cumpleaños feliz, cumpleaños feliz,	*Happy birthday to you, happy birthday to you,*
te deseamos todos cumpleaños feliz.	*we all wish you happy birthday.*
Pide un **deseo**.	Make a **wish**.
Sopla **las velas**.	Blow out the **candles**.
Sopla más fuerte.	Blow harder.
¡Bien! ¿Quién quiere tarta?	Good! Who wants cake?
¿Tú quieres tarta? ¿Sí?	Do you want some? Yes?
¡Es de chocolate!	*It's a chocolate cake!*
¿Quieres **un trozo grande** o **pequeño**?	Would you like a **big** or **small piece**?

Una tarta

Unas velas

Un trozo grande

Un trozo pequeño

¡Vamos a la playa!

Let's Go to the Beach!

En la playa

¡**La arena** está caliente!
No te quites **las sandalias**.
Saca **la toalla** de tu **mochila**.
Estira la toalla sobre la arena.
Ven que te pongo **el protector solar**.
No quiero que te quemes.
Un poquito en la cara.
Ahora en los brazos y en las piernas.
Los deditos de los pies.
¡Espera! No te vayas. ¡Ven aquí!
Ponte **la gorra** que el sol está
    muy fuerte.
Ayúdame a hacer un hoyo para
    la sombrilla.
¿Me prestas tu pala?
Cavo, cavo y cavo.
Y ahora, ¡al agua!
Ponte **el flotador**.

At the Beach

The **sand** is hot!
Don't take off your **sandals**.
Take the **towel** from your **backpack**.
Spread the towel on the sand.
Come here, I'll put some **sunscreen** on you.
I don't want you to get burned.
A little bit on your face.
Now on your arms and on your legs.
Your little toes.
Wait! Don't go away. Come here!
Put on your **cap**, the sun is
    very strong.
Help me make a hole for
    the **umbrella**.
Can I borrow your shovel?
I am digging, digging, and digging.
And now, to the water!
Put on your **inner tube**.

Did You Know?

You can set up a "beach" in the playroom or the backyard. Make a sun with construction paper. Mark off a pretend swimming area with tape. You can make a sandbox with a large container filled with sand and toys. Use a beach bag with beach towels, sand toys, and sunscreen. Have fun!

Las sandalias

El protector solar

La sombrilla

El flotador

Castillos de arena

Sand Castles

Vamos a hacer **un castillo de arena**.	Let's make a **sand castle**.
Aquí está **el balde**.	Here is the **bucket**.
Aquí está **la pala**.	Here is the **shovel**.
Llena el balde con arena.	Fill the bucket with sand.
Ahora, dalo vuelta.	Now, flip it over.
Palméalo suavecito.	Pat it softly.
Pan duro que se ponga blando.	*Hard bread, soften up.*
Pan duro que se ponga blando.	*Hard bread, soften up.*
Pan duro que se ponga blando.	*Hard bread, soften up.*
Ahora levanta el balde. ¡Despacio!	Now lift the bucket. Slowly!
¡Qué lindo!	*How beautiful!*
Elige **un molde** para hacer la torre.	Choose a **mold** to build a tower.
Llénalo de arena.	Fill it with sand.
Dalo vuelta despacito.	Flip it very slowly.
Toma **el rastrillo** y hazle un camino.	Take the **rake** and make a path.
Ahora, alísalo con la mano.	Now, smooth it with your hand.
Toma la pala y cava **un foso**.	Take the shovel and dig a **moat**.
¡No tires arena!	Don't throw sand!
¡Mira! Aquí tienes **conchas** y **piedras** para decorar el castillo.	Look! Here you have **shells** and **stones** to decorate the castle.
¡Qué castillo más lindo!	*What a beautiful castle!*

Un castillo de arena

Un balde

Una pala

Un rastrillo

En la primavera
In the Spring

Los movimientos de la primavera

El caracol, el caracol
se mueve muy despacio.
Muévete despacio como el caracol.
La mariposa, la mariposa
revolotea entre **las flores**.
Revolotea entre las flores como
    la mariposa.
La rana, la rana
salta en **el agua**.
Salta en el agua como la rana.
La mariquita, la mariquita
es muy chiquitita.
Eres chiquitito/a como la mariquita.
El viento, el viento
sopla y sopla.
Sopla como el viento.
La flor, la flor
se menea en el viento.
Menéate como una flor.
¡Llegó la primavera!

Spring's Movements

The **snail**, the snail
moves very slowly.
Move slowly like the snail.
The **butterfly**, the butterfly
flutters among the **flowers**.
Flutter among the flowers like
    the butterfly.
The **frog**, the frog
jumps in the **water**.
Jump in the water like the frog.
The **ladybug**, the ladybug
is very small.
You are small like the ladybug.
The **wind**, the wind
blows and blows.
Blow like the wind.
The flower, the flower
waves in the wind.
Wave like a flower.
Spring is here!

Did You Know?

"Que llueva" is a traditional song in Spain and Latin America. The song's text and tune vary from country to country. The version used here is from Spain. You may want to explain to your child that seasons are different in the northern and southern hemispheres. If you were to travel to South America in the spring, it would look like fall there!

Un caracol

Una mariposa

Una rana

Una mariquita

La lluvia

The Rain

¡Está lloviendo! Ponte **las botas**.
Ahora **el chubasquero**.
Vamos a abrir **los paraguas**.
¡Cómo llueve! ¡Es **un chaparrón**!
　　¡Vamos a cantar!
Que llueva, que llueva.
La Virgen de la cueva.
***Los pajaritos** cantan.*
***Las nubes** se levantan.*
¡Que sí!
¡Que no!
¡Que caiga un chaparrón
con azúcar y turrón!
¡Que se rompan los cristales de
　　la estación!
¡Vamos a saltar en **el charco**!
Ha parado de llover. *¡Qué bien huele!*
Es el olor de la primavera.

It's raining! Put on your **boots**.
Now the **raincoat**.
Let's open the **umbrellas**.
What a rain! It's a **downpour**!
　　Let's sing!
Let it rain, let it rain.
The Virgin of the cave.
*The **little birds** are singing.*
*The **clouds** rise up.*
Yes!
No!
Let the downpour fall
with sugar and sweets!
Let the windows of
　　the station break!
Let's jump in the **puddle**!
It stopped raining. *It smells so good!*
It's the smell of spring.

Las botas

El chubasquero

El paraguas

Las nubes

A pescar

Let's Go Fishing

¡Shhhh! Silencio.
Vamos a ver si hay peces.
Tira pan. Así, más migas.
Hay muchos peces.
Toma tu **caña de pescar**.
Pon el cebo en **el anzuelo**.
Lanza **el anzuelo**. Estupendo.
Vamos a esperar.
¡Ha picado algo!
Sujeta la caña fuerte y tira. ¡Tira!
*Es **una bota**. ¡Puaj!*
Pon más **cebo** y lanza el anzuelo.
¡Ha picado algo!
Sujeta la caña fuerte y tira. ¡Tira!
*¡Guau! Es **un pez gigante**.*
Debe ser el rey de los peces.
Ponlo en **la cesta**.
Pon más cebo y lanza el anzuelo.
¡Ha picado algo!
Es una lata. ¡Puaj!
¡Al menos es **una lata de sardinas**!

Shhhh! Silence!
We are going to see if there are fish.
Throw bread. Like this, more crumbs.
There are many fish.
Take your **fishing pole**.
Put the bait on the **hook**.
Cast the **line**. Great.
Let's wait.
Something bit!
Hold your pole tight and pull. Pull!
*It's a **boot**. Yikes!*
Put on more **bait** and cast the line.
Something bit!
Hold your pole tight and pull. Pull!
*Wow! It's a **giant fish**.*
It must be the king of fish.
Put it in the **basket**.
Put on more bait and cast the line.
Something bit!
It's a can. Yikes!
At least it's a **can of sardines**!

Did You Know?

Throw a blue tablecloth on the floor and use a large box or a coffee table placed upside down as a boat. For the fishing activity, place a few objects in the "river" and try to fish them out with a pole made with a stick and cord. (You may want to attach magnets to the pole and the objects you're fishing for.) Show a picture or a puppet of a wave, crocodile, and waterfall for the song.

La caña de pescar

El anzuelo

Un pez gigante

Una lata de sardinas

Por el río

By the River

Note: After each verse, repeat the *estribillo*/chorus.

Estribillo:
En mi **barca** remo.
Por el río voy,
por el río voy, por el río voy.

¡Viene **una ola** enorme!
¡Que viene la ola! ¡Que viene la ola!
¡Tápate la nariz!
Una ola viene acá.
Menos mal que ya se va. *(Estribillo)*

¡Viene **un cocodrilo**!
¡Rema deprisa, deprisa!
¡Que viene un cocodrilo!
¡Que viene un cocodrilo!
Un cocodrilo viene acá.
Menos mal que ya se va. *(Estribillo)*

¡Viene **una cascada**!
¿Qué hacemos, qué hacemos?
¡Viene una cascada!
Una cascada viene acá.
Menos mal que ya se va. *(Estribillo)*

Chorus:
In my **boat** I row.
By the river I go,
by the river I go, by the river I go.

A huge **wave** is coming!
The wave is coming! The wave is coming!
Cover your nose!
A wave is coming here.
Good thing it's going away. *(Chorus)*

A **crocodile** is coming!
Row fast, row fast!
A crocodile is coming!
A crocodile is coming!
A crocodile is coming here.
Good thing it's going away. *(Chorus)*

A **waterfall** is coming!
What do we do, what do we do?
A waterfall is coming!
A waterfall is coming here.
Good thing it's going away. *(Chorus)*

Una barca

Una ola

Un cocodrilo

Una cascada

En el otoño

In the Fall

Los esqueletos

The Skeletons

Note: After each hour, repeat the *estribillo*/chorus "Tumba, tumba, tumba-la-ca-tumba, tumba, tumba, tumba-la-ca-tún."

Cuando **el reloj** marca la una,
los esqueletos salen de la tumba.
Cuando el reloj marca las dos,
los esqueletos miran **el reloj**.
Cuando el reloj marca las tres,
los esqueletos se tocan **los pies**.
Cuando el reloj marca las cuatro,
los esqueletos se limpian **los zapatos**.
Cuando el reloj marca las cinco,
los esqueletos montan **en triciclo**.
Cuando el reloj marca las seis,
los esqueletos montan en **un tren**.
Cuando el reloj marca las siete,
los esqueletos van **en patinete**.
Cuando el reloj marca las ocho,
los esqueletos van en sus **motos**.
Cuando el reloj marca las nueve,
los esqueletos **ya no se mueven**.
Cuando el reloj marca las diez,
los esqueletos **ya no se ven**.
Cuando el reloj marca las once,
los esqueletos **ya no se oyen**.
Cuando el reloj marca las doce,
los esqueletos roncan en **la noche**.

When the **clock** strikes one,
the **skeletons** get out of their tombs.
When the clock strikes two,
the skeletons look at the **clock**.
When the clock strikes three,
the skeletons touch their **feet**.
When the clock strikes four,
the skeletons polish their **shoes**.
When the clock strikes five,
the skeletons ride their **tricycles**.
When the clock strikes six,
the skeletons ride on a **train**.
When the clock strikes seven,
the skeletons ride on **scooters**.
When the clock strikes eight,
the skeletons ride on their **motorcycles**.
When the clock strikes nine,
the skeletons **don't move**.
When the clock strikes ten,
the skeletons **can't be seen**.
When the clock strikes eleven,
the skeletons **can't be heard**.
When the clock strikes twelve,
the skeletons snore in the **night**.

Un esqueleto

El triciclo

El tren

El patinete

Una bruja mala

A Bad Witch

Una bruja mala camina por detrás.
Cierra bien los ojos.
¡Ábrelos, verás!
¡Corre, corre! ¡Atrapa a la bruja!
¡Bien! ¡La atrapaste!
Un brujo malo camina por detrás.
Cierra bien los ojos.
¡Ábrelos, verás!
¡Corre, corre! ¡Atrapa al brujo!
¡Bien! ¡Lo atrapaste!
Un fantasma malo camina por detrás.
Cierra bien los ojos.
¡Ábrelos, verás!
¡Corre, corre! ¡Atrapa al fantasma!
¡Bien! ¡Lo atrapaste!
Un monstruo malo camina por detrás.
Cierra bien los ojos.
¡Ábrelos, verás!
¡Corre, corre! ¡Atrapa al monstruo!
¡Bien! ¡Lo atrapaste!

A bad **witch** is walking behind us.
Close your eyes tight.
Open them, you'll see!
Run, run! Catch the witch!
Great! You caught her!
A bad **wizard** is walking behind us.
Close your eyes tight.
Open them, you'll see!
Run, run! Catch the wizard!
Great! You caught him!
A bad **ghost** is walking behind us.
Close your eyes tight.
Open them, you'll see!
Run, run! Catch the ghost!
Great! You caught him!
A bad **monster** is walking behind us.
Close your eyes tight.
Open them, you'll see!
Run, run! Catch the monster!
Great! You caught him!

La moto

Una bruja

Un fantasma

Un monstruo

En el invierno
In the Winter

La tormenta de nieve

The Snowstorm

Hace mucho frío.
¡Uy! ¡Qué frío!
¡Qué f-f-f-río!
Tengo mucho frío.
¿Y tú? ¿Tienes frío?
Yo tengo mucho frío.
Mira, está nevando.
¡Qué bonito!
¡Está nevando! *¡Qué bien!*
Toca **la nieve**.
¡Qué fría es la nieve!
¡Uy! ¡Qué fría!
¡Qué f-f-f-ría!
Vamos a hacer **bolas de nieve**.
Coge un poco de nieve. *Así.*
Haz una bola. *Así.*
Uno, dos, tres…
¡Tírala!
¡Oye!
¡Te di!

It is very cold.
Oh! How cold it is!
How c-c-c-old!
I am very cold.
What about you? Are you cold?
I am very cold.
Look, it is snowing.
How beautiful!
It is snowing! *Great!*
Touch the **snow**.
How cold is the snow!
Oh! How cold it is!
How c-c-c-old!
Let's make some **snowballs**.
Get some snow. *Like this.*
Make a ball. *Like this.*
One, two, three . . .
Throw it!
Hey!
Got you!

Did You Know?

You may want to explain to your child that while children in North America are making snowmen, in South America they are building sand castles. While in the northern hemisphere the winter months are January, February, and March, in the southern hemisphere they are July, August, and September. Many fresh fruits eaten in the United States during the winter months are imported from Argentina and Chile.

La tormenta de nieve

Una bola grande

Una bola mediana

Una bola pequeña

El muñeco de nieve

The Snowman

Note: Repeat the *estribillo*/chorus after each verse.

Estribillo:
Un muñeco de nieve soy
y en invierno bailo mejor.

Una bola ¡grande!
Una bola ¡mediana!
Y *otra más ¡pequeña!*
Para la cabeza. *(Estribillo)*

Muevo así *¡los brazos!*
Muevo así *¡los pies!*
Muevo así *¡el sombrero!*
Uno, dos y tres. *(Estribillo)*

¡Uy, no! ¡Salió el sol!
¡Qué calor, qué calor, qué calor!
¡Me derrito! ¡Me derrito!
Un charquito de agua soy.
Chapotea en mí: chop, chop, chop.
   (Estribillo)

Chorus:
I am a **snowman**
and I dance better in winter.

*A **big ball**!*
*A **medium-sized ball**!*
*And a **small ball**!*
For the head. *(Chorus)*

I move *my **arms*** like this!
I move *my **feet*** like this!
I move *my **hat*** like this!
One, two, and three. *(Chorus)*

Oh, no! The sun came out!
It is so hot, so hot, so hot!
I am melting! I am melting!
I am a **little puddle of water**.
Splash in me: splash, splash, splash.
   (Chorus)

Los brazos

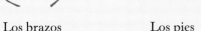

Los pies

El sombrero

El charquito de agua

Uso tecnología
I Use Technology

Vamos a poner fotos en Facebook

Let's Post Pictures on Facebook

Vamos a poner **fotos** en **Facebook**.
¿Las de mi cumple?
Sí, puedes elegir **tus diez favoritas**.
Vamos a buscarlas.
¿Qué fotos te gustan?
Me gusta en la que tiro la tarta.
Muy bien, ¿y qué tal en la que estás
    con **tu excavadora**?
¡Sí! Y esta también.
Ya tenemos diez.
Vamos a ponerlas en **un álbum**.
¡Mira! **La abuela** ha puesto
    un comentario.
Lo voy a leer.
"¡Me encanta ese avión!
    ¿Quién te lo ha regalado?"
Mami, dile que Juan me lo ha dado.
    Él es mi mejor, mejor, mejor amigo
    en el mundo entero.
¡Ah, **el abuelo** también ha escrito!
Dice que quiere jugar con tu
    excavadora.
¡Vale! Dile que jugaré con él.

Let's post **pictures** on **Facebook**.
The ones from my birthday?
Yes, you can choose **your ten favorites**.
Let's look for them.
What pictures do you like?
I like the one when I dropped the cake.
Okay, and what about the one
    with **your bulldozer**?
Yes! And this one too.
We have ten now.
Let's put them in an **album**.
Look! **Grandma** posted
    a **comment**.
Let me read it.
"I love that airplane!
    Who gave you that?"
Mom, say that Jack gave it to me.
    He's my best, best, best friend
    in the whole world.
Oh, **Grandpa** also wrote!
He says that he wants to play with your
    bulldozer.
Sure! Tell him that I'll play with him.

Una foto

Una excavadora

Facebook

Encender

Hablamos con los primos

We Talk with Our Cousins

¿Quieres hablar con **los primos**?
¡Vale!
Pues acércame **la computadora portátil**.
*Yo la **enciendo**.*
*¡Hola, **tía**! ¿Dónde estás?*
En **el parque**.
¿Quieres hablar con los primos?
Sí, sí. Quiero hablar con Mónica.
¡Hola, Mónica! ¿Qué estás haciendo?
*Estoy hablando contigo **por Skype**.*
¡No me digas! ¿Y qué más?
*Estoy montando en **mi bici nueva**.*
   ¿Quieres verla?
Sí, acerca la computadora.
*¡Oh, pero la mía es **más grande**!*
¡No te oigo!
¡No toques ese botón!
¡Vaya, se ha desconectado!
   Lo volveremos a intentar **más tarde**.
¡Aj!
Mientras tanto podemos jugar con
   el **iPod**.

Do you want to talk with **your cousins**?
Sure!
Then pass me **the laptop**.
*I'll **turn it on**.*
*Hello, **Auntie**! Where are you?*
At the **park**.
Do you want to talk with your cousins?
Yes, yes. I want to talk with Monica.
Hi, Monica! What are you doing?
*I'm talking with you **on Skype**.*
No kidding! And what else?
*I'm riding **my new bike**.*
   Do you want to see it?
Yes, bring the computer closer.
*Oh, but mine is **bigger**!*
I don't hear you!
Don't touch that button!
Oh, no, we lost the connection!
   We'll try again **later**.
Agh!
Meanwhile, we can play with
   the **iPod**.

La computadora
portátil

Los primos

La tía

iPod

En la ciudad

In the City

Año Nuevo en el barrio chino

New Year's in Chinatown

Papi, ¿qué es eso?
Es un desfile de **dragones**.
¿Quieres ir allí?
¡Sí, quiero verlo!
Agarra mi mano fuerte.
Hay muchísima **gente**.
*¿Qué es ese **ruido**?*
Es gente que toca **los tambores**
    para el Baile de los Dragones.
Y esos de ahí son **los leones**.
¿Y qué están haciendo?
Están celebrando el Año Nuevo Chino.
Cuando yo era niño en China, **los**
    abuelos siempre me daban **un**
    sobre rojo para el Año Nuevo.
¿Y qué había dentro del sobre?
Dinero.
Significa **buena suerte** para el
    nuevo año.

Dad, what's that?
It's a **dragon** parade.
Do you want to go there?
Yes, I want to see it!
Hold my hand tight.
There are too many **people**.
*What's that **noise**?*
It's people playing the **drums**
    for the Dragon Dance.
And those over there are the **lions**.
And what are they doing?
They are celebrating Chinese New Year.
When I was a little boy in China, **Grandma**
    and Grandpa always gave me **a**
    red envelope for the New Year.
And what was inside the envelope?
Money.
It means **good luck** for the
    New Year.

Did You Know?

When children learn a new language, they develop academic, intercultural, and language-learning abilities that will serve them well no matter what the future brings in terms of studies, jobs, business opportunities, personal interests, or travel. There is no crystal ball that can predict which language will be most useful for your child in the future. Not to worry! Learning a new language trains your brain to learn languages in general.

Un dragón

Un tambor

Un sobre rojo

Dinero

Comiendo en la ciudad

Eating in the City

Tengo hambre. ¡Quiero comer ya!

Sí. Vamos a mirar los puestos de comida. Hay comida china, pizza, **hamburguesas** y perritos calientes, bocadillos…

¿Qué quieres?

*Quiero **pizza sin nada**.*

Vale. ¿Y qué quieres **beber**?

*Hay jugo, **agua**, limonada, Coca-Cola…*

Coca-Cola, por favor.

*Mami, ¡tienen **las frutas** que te gustan!*

"Ensalada de kiwis". ¡Mmm!

Suena interesante.

Probaré una.

Vamos a sentarnos en **esa mesa**.

¿Qué quieren hacer ahora?

¿Por qué no tomamos **un autobús de dos pisos**?

*¡Sí, sí, **en el piso de arriba**!*

Ahí está **la parada del autobús.**

¡Corran, viene un autobús!

I'm hungry. I want to eat now!

Yes. Let's check the food stands. There's Chinese food, pizza, **hamburgers** and hot dogs, sandwiches . . .

What do you want?

*I want **plain pizza**.*

Okay. And what do you want **to drink**?

There's juice, **water**, lemonade, Coke . . .

Coke, please.

*Mommy, they have the **fruit** that you like!*

"Kiwi salad." Mmm!

That seems interesting.

I'll try one.

Let's sit at **that table**.

What do you want to do now?

Why don't we ride **a double-decker bus**?

*Yes, yes, **in the upper deck**!*

The **bus stop** is there.

Run, a bus is coming!

Agua

Frutas

Una hamburguesa

Un autobús de dos pisos

En la escuela
At School

El primer día de escuela

The First Day of School

Hola, ¿cómo te llamas?	Hello, what's your name?
Ani.	*Annie.*
Yo soy la señorita García.	I'm Miss García.
Bienvenida a nuestra clase.	**Welcome** to our classroom.
Ahora que ya estamos todos aquí, vamos a sentarnos en **un círculo**.	Now that we're all here, let's sit in a **circle**.
Hoy vamos a hablar de nuestras cosas favoritas.	Today, we are going to talk about our favorite things.
¿Pueden adivinar mi **color** favorito?	Can you guess my favorite **color**?
¡Azul!	*Blue!*
¡Rojo!	*Red!*
¡Amarillo!	*Yellow!*
¡Naranja!	*Orange!*
No, ¡es el **morado**!	Nope, it's **purple**!
Ahora **es su turno** de hablar de sus **juguetes** favoritos.	Now **it's your turn** to tell us about your favorite **toys**.
¿Cuál es tu juguete favorito, Juan?	Which is your favorite toy, John?
El iPhone de mi mamá.	*My mom's iPhone.*
¿Y por qué te gusta el iPhone de tu mamá?	And why do you like your mom's iPhone?
*Porque puedo **tocar el piano** y puedo hablar con mi papá.*	*Because I can **play piano** and I can talk with my daddy.*
¿Y **el tuyo**, Vera?	And **yours**, Valerie?
*A mí me gustan mis **bloques** nuevos.*	*I like my new **blocks**.*
¡Son grandísimos!	*They're huge!*
¿Ah, sí? ¿Y qué has construido con ellos?	Oh, yes? What have you built with them?
*Un **castillo** enorme para mi dragón.*	*An enormous **castle** for my dragon.*

Azul

Rojo

Amarillo

Naranja o anaranjado

¡Vamos a hacer matemáticas!

Let's Do Math!

¡Buenos días, clase!

Hoy vamos a contar cosas **juntos**.

¿Cuántas **niñas** hay en la clase, María?

Cuéntalas a ver.

Una, dos, tres, cuatro, cinco, seis, siete.

¡Correcto, hay siete niñas en la clase!

Y ahora, ¿cuántas **galletas** creen que hay en **el tarro de las galletas**?

¡Doce!

¡Treinta y siete!

Vamos a ver...

¡Oh, no! ¡**Cero**!

¿Quién se ha comido las galletas?

¡Yo no!

Robertito… ¿qué tienes en las manos?

¿Nos puedes decir cuántas galletas había en el tarro de galletas?

No sé.

Bueno, ¡pues **la próxima vez** asegúrate de contarlas antes de comértelas, ja, ja!

Good morning, class!

Today we are going to count things **together**.

How many **girls** are in the class, Mary?

Count them and see.

One, two, three, four, five, six, seven.

Correct, there are seven girls in the class!

And now, how many **cookies** do you think there are in the **cookie jar**?

Twelve!

Thirty-seven!

Let's see . . .

¡Oh, no! **Zero**!

Who ate the cookies?

Not me!

Bobby . . . what's that in your hands?

Can you tell us how many cookies there were in the cookie jar?

I don't know.

Well, **next time** make sure you at least count them before eating them, ha, ha!

Uno o una

Dos

Tres

Cuatro

Quiero a mis mascotas
I Love My Pets

Quiero un gatito

I Want a Kitty

*Mami, mi amiga Lisa tiene
    un gatito nuevo.*
¡Yo también quiero uno!
Pero ya tenemos un pequeño zoo aquí.
Veamos:
Un perro,
tres **ranas,**
dos **hámsters,**
una tortuga
y **una lagartija.**
*¡Pero me gustaría tener **un gato**!*
Y los gatitos pequeñitos son tan lindos...
Sí, pero luego crecen.
¿Y dónde va a dormir el gatito?
En mi cama.
¿Y quién le va a dar de comer?
Yo.
¿Y quién va a limpiar el cajón con
    la caca y **el pis**?
Mami, qué asco. Eso no me gusta.
¿Ves?
De todas maneras papá **tiene alergia
    a** los gatos.
*¡Pues que papi no entre en **mi cuarto**!*
¡Pobre papi!
No podemos tener un gatito, pero
    podemos ir a jugar con el de Lisa
    cuando quieras.
*Bueno, ¡**vámonos**!*

*Mommy, my friend Lisa has
    a new kitty.*
I want one too!
But we already have a small zoo here.
Let's see:
One dog,
three **frogs,**
two **hamsters,**
one turtle,
and **one lizard**.
*But I'd like to have **a cat**!*
And little kittens are so cute . . .
Yes, but then they grow up.
And where is the kitty going to sleep?
In my bed.
And who is going to feed him?
I will.
And who is going to clean the box with
    the **poop** and **pee**?
Mommy, that's yucky. I don't like that.
See?
Anyway, Daddy **is allergic
    to** cats.
*Then Daddy doesn't have to go into **my room**!*
Poor Daddy!
We can't have a kitty, but
    we can go play with Lisa's
    whenever you want.
Okay, **let's go**!

Un hámster

Una tortuga

Una lagartija

Un gato

Mi perro va a la escuela canina

My Dog Goes to Dog School

*Papi, ¿**por qué** tiene que ir Max a la escuela?*

Porque necesita aprender matemáticas.

¡Es broma! Porque tiene que **aprender** a escuchar.

¡Hola! Soy el **adiestrador** de perros.

¿Cómo se llama tu **perro**?

Max.

Hola, Max. Vamos a ver qué puedes hacer.

Max, ¡**siéntate**!

¡Oh, no, Max! ¡No te vayas!

Tienes que escuchar al adiestrador.

Max, ¡camina **conmigo**!

¡Buen chico, Max!

Voy a tirar **este palo**.

Ahora, Max, ¡ve a buscarlo!

*Max, ¡**corre de prisa**! ¡Ve, ve, ve!*

¡Bien! ¡Lo ha cogido!

*Daddy, **why** does Max need to go to school?*

Because he needs to learn his math.

I'm just kidding! Because he needs **to learn** how to listen.

Hi! I'm the dog **trainer**.

What's your **dog's** name?

Max.

Hi, Max. Let's see what you can do.

Max, **sit**!

Oh, no, Max! Don't walk away!

You have to listen to your trainer.

Max, walk **with me**!

Good boy, Max!

I'm going to throw **this stick**.

Now, Max, go fetch!

*Max, **run fast**! Go, go, go!*

Yay! He got it!

Un perro

Caca

¡Siéntate!

¡Corre!

Nos vamos de viaje

We're Going on a Trip

En el aeropuerto

Pasaportes, por favor.

¿Adónde viajan hoy?

A Cuzco, Perú.

Gracias.

Aquí están sus pasaportes.

Y estos tickets son para **las maletas**.

¡Buen viaje!

Quítate **los zapatos** y ponlos en
    el cajón.

¿Adónde vamos?

Vamos a **la puerta de embarque**.

Quiero ir al cuarto de baño.

Espera a que encontremos nuestros
    asientos.

Fila treinta y dos.

¡Aquí están nuestros **asientos**!

¡Este cuarto de baño es enano, papi!

*Nuestro cuarto de baño en casa es
    más grande que éste.*

At the Airport

Passports, please.

Where are you traveling today?

To Cuzco, Peru.

Thank you.

Here are your passports.

And these tickets are for **the suitcases**.

Have a good trip!

Take **your shoes** off and put them in
    the bucket.

Where are we going?

We're going to the **boarding gate**.

I want to go to the bathroom.

Wait until we find our
    seats.

Row thirty-two.

Here are our **seats**!

This bathroom is tiny, Daddy!

*Our bathroom at home is
    much bigger than this.*

Did You Know?

The Incas once ruled one of the largest and richest empires in Latin America. With its capital in Cuzco (Peru), the Inca Empire covered much of present-day Ecuador, Peru, Bolivia, Chile, and parts of Colombia and Argentina. Quechua was the Incas' language, and some Quechua words are used in English and Spanish today, including "condor," "gaucho," "Inca," "lima" (bean), "llama," "pampa," "puma," and "vicuña." The Inca Empire ended with the invading Spanish conquistadors in the sixteenth century.

El pasaporte

El cuarto de baño

El asiento

Las maletas

En el hotel

¿*Vamos a dormir aquí* **esta noche**?

Sí, y mañana saldremos **pronto** para ir
a Machu Picchu.

¿Te has lavado **los dientes**?

Sí.

Pues **vete a la cama** entonces.

Vamos a salir pronto, así que
intenta dormir. ¡Buenas noches!

***

¡Despierta!

Tenemos que prepararnos para tomar
el autobús de turismo.

¡Boletos, por favor! Gracias.

¿***Falta mucho?***

Deja de preguntar. Ya casi estamos.

¡Mira! ¿Puedes ver **las murallas**?

¿*Dónde? ¿Dónde?*

¡Ahí, arriba en **la montaña**!

¡*Guau!* ¿*Y* **quién** *vive ahí?*

Nadie, son todo **ruinas,** pero antes
vivían ahí los incas.

¿***Quiénes eran*** *los incas?*

Eran indios nativos del Perú que hace
cinco siglos…

At the Hotel

Are we going to sleep here **tonight**?

Yes, and tomorrow we'll leave **early** to go
to Machu Picchu.

Did you brush your **teeth**?

Yes.

Go to bed then.

We're going to leave early, so
try to sleep. Good night!

***

Wake up!

We have to get ready to take
the tour bus.

Tickets, please! Thank you.

Are we there yet?

Stop asking. We're almost there.

Look! Can you see **the walls**?

Where? Where?

Over there, up on **the mountain**!

Wow! And **who** *lives there?*

Nobody, it's all **ruins,** but a long time ago
the Incas lived there.

Who were the Incas?

They were the native Indians of Peru,
five hundred years ago, who . . .

El autobús

El hotel

La montaña

Las murallas

Juegos
Games

En mi casa

¿Qué hay **en el garaje**?
*Hay **un coche**.*
*Hay **una bicicleta**.*
*Hay **un tractor**.*

¿Qué pasa **en el portal**?
*Hay una señora **saliendo del** ascensor.*
*Hay un señor **paseando a** su perro.*
*Hay un niño **llorando**.*

¿Qué hacen las personas **en el gimnasio**?
*Una señora **levanta** pesas.*
*Un señor **corre** en la cinta.*
*Unos niños **juegan al** baloncesto.*

¿Qué sucede **en la sala de estar**?
*El abuelo **mira la tele con** su nieto.*
*La abuela **le lee un cuento a** su nieta.*
*El bebé **juega con** su osito.*

¿Qué hacen los adultos **en la cocina**?
*El padre **está secando** los platos.*
*La madre **está cocinando**.*
*La vecina **está hablando** sin parar.*

¿Qué pasa **en el comedor**?
*El papá **quiere** más agua.*
*La abuela **se está comiendo** todos los espaguetis.*
*La mamá **está muy enfadada**.*

¿Qué hay **en el cuarto**?
*Hay **una cama** roja.*
*Hay **un armario** lleno de ropa.*
*Hay **un escritorio** y libros.*

¿Qué pasa **en el baño**?
*La madre **se está peinando**.*
*El niño **se está lavando los dientes**.*
*La niña pequeña **está haciendo pis y caca**.*

¿A qué juegan los niños **en el cuarto de los juguetes**?
***Las niñas** juegan con sus muñecas.*
***El niño mayor** juega con bloques.*
***El niño pequeño** juega con su tren.*

In My House

What's **in the garage**?
*There's a **car**.*
*There's a **bicycle**.*
*There's a **tractor**.*

What's happening **in the lobby**?
*There's a woman **getting out of** the elevator.*
*There's a man **walking** his dog.*
*There's a boy **crying**.*

What are the people doing **in the gym**?
*A woman **lifts** weights.*
*A man **runs** on the treadmill.*
*Some children **play** basketball.*

What's going on **in the living room**?
*The grandpa **watches TV with** his grandson.*
*The grandma **reads a story to** her granddaughter.*
*The baby **plays with** his teddy bear.*

What are the adults doing **in the kitchen**?
*The father **is drying** the dishes.*
*The mother **is cooking**.*
*The neighbor **is talking** nonstop.*

What's happening **in the dining room**?
*The dad **wants** more water.*
*The grandma **is eating** all the spaghetti.*
*The mom **is very angry**.*

What's **in the bedroom**?
*There's a red **bed**.*
*There's a **closet** full of clothes.*
*There's a **desk** and books.*

What's happening **in the bathroom**?
*The mother **is combing her hair**.*
*The boy **is brushing his teeth**.*
*The little girl **is making pee and poop**.*

What are the children playing **in the playroom**?
***The girls** are playing with their dolls.*
***The older boy** is playing with blocks.*
***The little boy** is playing with his train.*

ow to Play the Game

his game is designed to be played as the traditional "Tic-Tac-Toe" game ("Tres en Raya" or "Ta-Te-Ti" in Spanish). The building in the large mage will be your board. The building is divided into three floors with three rooms each, just as the typical 3 × 3 boxes on a "Tic-Tac-Toe" oard are. As you play the game, you can get extra vocabulary practice by asking each player to say something about the room before he or he puts a token down. Therefore, it is a good idea to practice the vocabulary *before* playing the game!

Here are several sample questions and answers you can use as prompts to get kids talking about the different scenes in the house.

Juegos
Games

En la clase de la señorita Calamidad...

Un niño disfrazado de **pirata** está saltando sobre la mesa. ¿Lo ves?

Hay **varios libros** en la estantería. ¿Cuántos? [Seis]

Hay **varios números** 4 escondidos. ¿Los ves?

¿De qué colores son **los columpios**? [Rojo y verde]

Al lado de la niña de la peluca roja hay **un basurero.** ¿Lo ves?

La señorita C está tocando **un instrumento**. ¿Cuál es? [Un trombón]

Hay dos niños **jugando al escondite**. ¿Los encuentras?

En **el caballete** hay un niño pintando con las manos. ¿Lo ves?

Hay **una suma** en **la pizarra**. ¿La ves?

Hay **un elefante** de **plastilina**. ¿Dónde está? [Debajo de **una silla**]

Otras cosas que puedes buscar:
Un tobogán
Un sube y baja
Una computadora
Una radio
Un iPod
Un cuaderno
Unos crayones
Unos marcadores
Unas tijeras
Un balón de baloncesto
Un avión
Un caballo

In Miss Calamity's Class . . .

A boy dressed as a **pirate** is jumping on the table. Do you see him?

There are **several books** on the bookshelf. How many? [Six]

There are **several number** 4s hidden. Do you see them?

What colors are the **swings**? [Red and green]

Beside the girl with the red wig there is a **trash can.** Do you see it?

Miss C is playing an **instrument**. Which one is it? [A trombone]

There are two boys **playing hide-and-seek**. Can you find them?

At the **easel** there's a boy painting with his hands. Do you see him?

There's an **addition problem** on the **board**. Do you see it?

There's a **play-dough elephant**. Where is it? [Under a **chair**]

Other things you can look for:
A slide
A seesaw
A computer
A radio
An iPod
A notebook
Crayons
Markers
Scissors
A basketball
An airplane
A horse

ow to Play the Game

is game is played in a similar fashion to "I Spy" ("Veo veo" in Spanish). Ask your child to find what you are talking about in the ustration. Feel free to use other questions or vocabulary.

About the Authors

Ana Lomba's breakthrough method "Ana Lomba's Easy Immersion®" is changing the way people think about and interact with young children learning languages. Ana's lively resources and detailed lesson plans are favorites with teachers and parents who want to nurture young children's innate language abilities. A Princeton University graduate, Ana has taught Spanish from preschool to college and held leadership positions with national language organizations in the United States. Ana is a native of Madrid, Spain, and she lives with her husband and three children in Princeton, New Jersey. For more information about Ana's teaching resources, e-storybook collections, and iPad applications, go to www. analomba.com.

Marcela Summerville is the founder of Spanish Workshop for Children, an award-winning Spanish immersion program for young children in Philadelphia. Marcela is also a workshop presenter sharing her innovative teaching methodology at prestigious conferences across North America. In addition, she has published articles on teaching a second language to youth. Marcela is a native of Patagonia, Argentina, and she lives with her husband and two children in Philadelphia. For more information, visit www. spanishworkshopforchildren.com.

Frank D. Jacobs

Pedro Pérez del Solar, a native of Peru, holds a Ph.D. in Spanish Literature and has been a press illustrator since 1990. Pedro is currently an assistant professor of Spanish Literature and Culture at the University of Texas at El Paso.